Praise for
MAGIC DUST

"Mark was with me at my very first real company, MicroSolutions. We built a team that went on to break new technological ground, but more importantly, we worked together to build a culture and organization that grew to eighty employees. That number isn't huge or spectacular, but what was unique is that out of the eighty, only one person quit and that person came back to work for us in a few months. That's how special MicroSolutions was. Mark provides insights to what made us work so well and more in his storied career."

—Mark Cuban, Entrepreneur and Investor on ABC's
Shark Tank, Owner of the Dallas Mavericks, Bestselling
Author of *How to Win at the Sport of Business*

"The most successful people simply lean on their most impactful abilities . . . That's precisely the lesson Mark Harris has distilled in *Magic Dust*: You were born with everything you need to reach your dreams, and the path is straightforward. Be yourself, as deeply as possible. This book offers an unmistakable guide for how to recognize your own Magic Dust and maximize its power it so you can create the most good."

—Josh Ellis, Editor-in-Chief at *Success*

"If you want to learn how to discover your own Magic Dust—read this book!"

—Vincent M. Roazzi, Author of
The Spirituality of Success: Getting Rich with Integrity

"Medical Alliance was a young, disruptive, fast-growing medical services company in desperate need of superstars to help lead our business. We were elated when Mark joined us and led our most important market to new heights. Mark is very smart and driven. His passion and demand for perfection and production made our entire company better."

—Paul Herchman, Founder and Former CEO of Medical Alliance

Magic Dust

Magic Dust

What Is It? Who Has It?
How Do You Get It?

Mark J. Harris

BROWN BOOKS
PUBLISHING GROUP

Magic Dust
What Is It? Who Has It? How Do You Get It?

Brown Books Publishing Group
Dallas, TX / New York, NY
www.BrownBooks.com
(972) 381-0009

A New Era in Publishing®

Publisher's Cataloging-In-Publication Data

Names: Harris, Mark J. (Mark John), 1963- author.
Title: Magic dust : What is it? Who has it? How do you get it? / Mark J. Harris.
Description: Dallas, TX ; New York, NY : Brown Books Publishing Group,
    [2021]
Identifiers: ISBN 9781612543321
Subjects: LCSH: Inspiration--Anecdotes. | Success--Anecdotes. | Self-
    actualization (Psychology)--Anecdotes. | Motivation (Psychology)--
    Anecdotes.
Classification: LCC BF410 .H37 2021 | DDC 153.3/02--dc23

ISBN 978-1-61254-332-1
LCCN 2021903191

Printed in Canada
10 9 8 7 6 5 4 3 2 1

To the memory of my lifelong friend, Greg Rump, who left this earth far too early.

To the memory of the three people mentioned in this book who died before its completion: Beau Williford, Terry Bjornsen, and Charles Terrell.

To the memory of my parents, John and JoAnn Harris, whom I look forward to seeing again in Heaven.

And to Morgan, Zoe, Abbie, Tanner, and Sophie, the children who call me "Dad," who inspired me and motivated me to complete this book.

CONTENTS

Part IV: Warriors   113

INTRODUCTION

When I began writing this book and compiling these profiles, I knew that I wanted to provide inspirational, motivational, entrepreneurial, and most of all heartfelt stories about people who had overcome great obstacles and achieved success in a variety of ways. I wanted the book to inspire others. Yet when I started, I had no idea how timely it would be. In a world dealing with the threat of COVID-19, in a nation where a thriving economy turned upside down almost overnight, I find these stories have particular relevance. And because I was focused on you, the reader, I had no idea how much writing this book would inspire me as well. I should have guessed, though, because the men and women I have profiled here have always inspired me.

In these pages, you will meet my heroes: the visionaries, the implementors, the motivators, and the warriors. All of them display that special quality I believe we all have—Magic Dust. When you read their stories, I want you to think about your own Magic Dust qualities. Don't worry about what category you "fit" in. No one fits in just one place throughout his or her life. Originally, I wanted to go to law school so that I could take on the big guys and fight for the little guys. But circumstances put me on a different path—one I will share with you later in this book.

Just know that it's OK to consider yourself an implementor sometimes and a visionary at other times. You may shift from any category to another. All that matters is that you identify *your* Magic Dust and, if necessary, adjust your path to move closer to your goals and your true values and desires.

In this book, you'll meet James Rodriguez, who had his whole life ripped out from under him. He could have been killed in his own country, but he invented a new life for himself in this one, where he and his wife have raised two amazing sons. You'll meet Brian Slipperjack-Baskatawang, my "fish whisperer" and a cancer survivor. You'll meet Mark Cuban, who was my boss during his early visionary days at MicroSolutions. You'll meet Paul Herchman, who offered me the opportunity to transition into healthcare. He dealt with major challenges, both physical and financial. He went from borrowing from friends to survive to selling a company for more than $80 million. You'll also meet collegiate basketball player and entrepreneur Erin Young Garrett; former NFL player Doug Dawson; Stephanie Nunez, my CFO for many years; and Tom Udstuen, who connected with me through Big Brothers and never let go. These are just a few of the people whose stories I hope will resonate with you. May their example put you even more firmly on the path you choose and with greater resolve than ever.

Your beginnings don't define your dreams. You do. Your Magic Dust does. That's why I wrote this book, even before I had any idea of what was ahead for our country and our world. May the stories you read here remind you of how strong you are. May they show you what is possible. And may they inspire you to take those next steps to get there.

—Mark J. Harris

Part I
VISIONARIES

Can you teach somebody how to be a visionary? I don't think so. I view that journey as more of a calling, something upon which you embark naturally. A visionary sees a need or a void in a service or product and tries to fill it with a solution. As Malcolm Gladwell said, "The visionary starts with a clean sheet of paper and reimagines the world."

Visionaries exist in all fields. Patti Smith defined them like this: "Artists, musicians, scientists—if you have any kind of visionary aptitude, it's often something you don't have a choice in. You have to do it."

We've all said, "I could have come up with that service," or "I had that same idea." The difference between having the idea and acting on it is what makes a visionary. A visionary is someone who acts on an idea and acts on it before anyone else does. Visionaries race to market to get the biggest share. They also race to market in second place to stake a claim on something that improves the flaws of the one who came in first.

Being a visionary is simply a matter of having the courage to put your foot in the ring. It's the willingness to step onto the playing floor or the field. In sports, we play the game because that's the only way we can truly know who will win. If we don't play, we will never know what situations might arise, and we will never know the outcome. Life is the same way. Visionaries are focused on outcomes.

I could name any number of successful visionaries, going all the way back to George Washington or even earlier. According to *Forbes*, the top ten innovators and leaders of 2019—with two familiar names sharing first place—are as follows:

1. Jeff Bezos and Elon Musk (Amazon and Tesla)
3. Mark Zuckerberg (Facebook)
4. Marc Benioff (Salesforce, *Time* magazine)
5. Reed Hastings (Netflix)
6. Satya Nadella (Microsoft)
7. Shantanu Narayen (Adobe)
8. Tim Cook (Apple)
9. Arne Sorenson (Marriott)
10. Larry Page and Sergey Brin (Google)

Many more visionaries are changing the world every day.

Early Lessons

While growing up in the Midwest, enduring months of snow and rain that kept us indoors, I had plenty of time to ponder the future. When I wasn't outside shoveling neighbors' cars out from under snow, I was dreaming of the summer, when I could mow lawns, detassel corn, and paint houses. I didn't come from wealth or privilege. My mom and dad married when she was sixteen and he was eighteen. My two sisters and I were born before she turned twenty-one. We learned early on that life was not fair, but we learned some other lessons too.

My early experience as a paperboy taught me some important life lessons, including the importance of dealing with tough customers who hold you accountable. One such customer was Mr. Thurston. He stood out on his lawn most days wearing the blue jean coveralls known in Iowa as bibs and a white tank top, the tattoos on both arms in clear sight. He had a cleanly shaved bald head, tobacco-worn teeth, and a rough voice from years of smoking. He may have been only five feet seven with a thin frame, but he was big enough to intimidate a young boy of ten or twelve who was just trying to deliver the paper each morning to his home. It was not required that the paper be delivered at a certain time of day to each customer, but Mr. Thurston had his time picked out. He decided that if the paper were not at his doorstep between 5:00 and 5:30 a.m., then he would assume it was not coming and call the newspaper company directly to complain.

And that wasn't all that bothered him. During the six months with mild weather, it was not difficult to land the paper on the four-by-four cement block under his front door. If the paper happened to land on a shrub or too far out of sight under the front door, Mr. Thurston was quick to call the newspaper company. His other request: on snowy or rainy days, he wanted his paper placed inside his screen door, where it would stay dry.

Needless to say, he was not a favorite customer on my route. Each month, when I had to collect payments from customers, he paid the newspaper directly, which left me no opportunity to befriend him or ease the tension his demands created.

Fast forward six or seven years after my paperboy days ended. One day, I was driving by his home. As usual, he was in his front yard, standing there swatting his newspaper from his right hand into his left. He yelled at me, "Hey, paperboy!" as I drove by.

I waved and said, "Hello, Mr. Thurston. How are you, sir?" He yelled again and told me to pull over. As I did so, he walked toward my car. My window was rolled down, since my car did not have a working AC unit for most of my high school and college years.

Mr. Thurston stood a few feet away from the curb where I had parked and said in his rougher-than-ever voice, "So you're the sports kid in the paper?"

Almost surprised, I replied, "I guess so, sir, yes."

He said, "I bet your parents are proud, huh?"

I replied, "I don't know, sir. I guess so and hope so."

He quickly said, less harshly, "So are your neighbors."

I sped home and immediately told my parents about my brief conversation with the most difficult customer I'd ever had in my first official job. There was a life lesson here that many of us learn early. The lesson was accountability. Not only did this man expect his paper on time, but he wanted it in a certain location. His satisfaction was important to me. He had a military background, and this had obviously taught him that it didn't matter how old I was. He had requirements he expected to be followed with no exceptions.

Thank you, Mr. Thurston, for being a mentor in those life lessons that this young man never forgot. Customer satisfaction is more than a catchphrase when your meager earnings depend on whether the guy who demands his paper on the front porch and on time is satisfied, especially if he wants a refund that comes out of your pocket.

After college, I relocated to Dallas, where I encountered numerous doors to opportunity. Drawn to computers and technology, I began my career. That's when I met Mark Cuban. So let's start right here with him.

Mark Cuban

MicroSolutions

"It's not about money or connections. It's the willingness
to outwork and outlearn everyone. And if it fails, you learn
from what happened and do a better job next time."

Most people think of Mark Cuban as an overnight success. To that, he
says: it doesn't matter how many times you fail; you have to be right
only once. When we worked together back in the MicroSolutions days,
he was already on his way.

A day in the life at MicroSolutions was all activity. Some might have
seen the company as organized chaos. When I joined, I encountered
nonstop moving parts and a team of people who were only in their
second year of doing business together. These circumstances could
have made it difficult to prioritize since there was so much going on,
but a big part of Mark Cuban's Magic Dust was getting people focused.

Mark and his partner Martin Woodall both had their own clients
already; plus, they were actively selling directly along with a crew of

system consultants (who functioned as sales people). "Sales cures all" was a mantra of Mark's. I adopted it as my own, and it was the ultimate Magic Dust.

Cuban grew up in a working-class family in the suburbs of Mt. Lebanon, Pennsylvania. At the age of twelve, he wanted a pair of expensive basketball shoes. He sold garbage bags door to door so he could buy them. You may have heard the story about how he managed to change his life completely. He had a bartending job right out of college and slept on the floor of an apartment he rented with other guys so he could buy a $99 computer. He taught himself programming and was hired by a company that sold PC software— only to be fired because he disobeyed his CEO, who told him to clean the office when Cuban said he was going to pick up a $15,000 check from a sale he had just made.

That's when, at age twenty-five, he started his own company, MicroSolutions. The guy with the $15,000 check was his first client. In an article for *Forbes*, Cuban describes those early days at MicroSolutions:

> I was a PC consultant, and I sold software and did training and configured computers. I wrote my own programs. I immersed myself in the PC industry and studied Microsoft and Lotus and watched what the smartest people did to make things work. I remember one day I had to drive to Austin for some PC part, to a place called PCs Limited. The place was run by this kid who was younger than I was. We sat down and talked for a few hours. I was really impressed by him. I remember telling him, "Dude, I think we're both going places." That "dude" was Michael Dell.[1]

1. Monte Burke, "At Age 25 Mark Cuban Learned Lessons About Leadership That Changed His Life," *Forbes*, March 28, 2013, https://www.forbes.com/sites/monteburke/2013/03/28/at-age-25-mark-cuban-learned-lessons-about-leadership-that-changed-his-life/.

Going places—and then some.

Lisa Lyles, a woman who's now deceased, referred me for an interview at MicroSolutions. She described the place as "a boutique company" that was "up and coming." Cuban was one of several players vying for a corner on the market of personal computers, as opposed to the older version of terminals tied to large mainframe computing machines. He needed to differentiate his company, and he did.

Cuban's goal was to gain attention in the marketplace and differentiate MicroSolutions from the next computer shop by using LAN (local area network) technology. Of course, LAN technology wasn't entirely new, but the idea of sharing files on personal computers and still having access to a mainframe was. This offered major opportunity in the mid-1980s.

LAN was my foot in the door when I went to talk to decision makers at companies like Dave & Buster's, Lincoln Property, and Trammell Crow. The pitch was basically this: "Hey, do you guys want to tie your computers together in local area networks and share files?" This was brand-new stuff back then, and its practical applications seemed limitless. Prior to that, people were just working with single-user PCs. The choice was either to go from a mainframe to a terminal or to have your computer act as a terminal with limited access. The concept of computers sharing files without having to go onto a mainframe was a big deal.

There I was, at age twenty-three, joining this iconic team in their second year of operation. I was sitting around a table with Cuban, his business partner Martin Woodall, Sally Racca, and Tony Cerbone. Tony had a master of business administration. Sally was an accomplished accountant and certified public accountant. As we sat around the table divvying up the top one hundred companies in Dallas–Fort Worth in a kind of "you pick one, I pick one" matchup, I could feel the focus. Mark Cuban was the let's-go-get-'em guy. "Here's the list," he would say. "Go make it happen."

We didn't sit there and strategize together, but when we met again, we'd talk about the calls we made and how they went. I felt I could talk to the others about my customer meetings and ask for their suggestions.

Martin Woodall was the detail guy. He used to do all the ordering; he made sure the inventory was coordinated and set up and that, when it got to the clients, the software was loaded. Mike Wininger was his go-to supervisor, in charge of service. Martin was more of a COO, while Mark was the president and sales guy. (When speaking of the CEO who fired him, Cuban writes in the *Forbes* piece, "Even now I think back to things he did, and I do the opposite. And he made me superstitious about titles. I'm never listed as the CEO of my companies. There is no CEO. I am the president.")

Scott Susans, another key team member, handled a lot of the programming and delivery details. Scott got to go out to California or Minnesota or New York or Chicago on a couple of trips for my clients.

I'm not sure what the revenue volume was when I arrived in 1986. Maybe the company was making something like $3 million in revenue. But I am pretty sure they were making over $10 million by year three. After my first quarter, the company offered a trip to Mexico for the highest revenue earner. The next thing I knew, I'd won the trip. Three months later, I won the next trip. Jim Kelley, my roommate, and Mike Wininger were my lucky travel companions.

In one of Mark Cuban's first books, he talks about incentivizing. That's what took place at MicroSolutions. We felt appreciated, and we felt part of something important, from the first person you talked to on the phone at MicroSolutions. Deb Colbert was memorable for her sweet Mesquite, Texas, accent and her always-polite phone etiquette. I recall how several of my customers commented about how cute her voice was and how friendly they felt our company was just based on her interactions with them over the phone.

When there was a discussion or disagreement—for instance, if a product was coming in and they had to split the product between clients—Mark and Martin would go into one of their offices and shut the door. Raised voices were normal when there was a closed-door discussion. Eventually, Mark would come out and say, "OK, this is what we're going to do."

When we went to happy hours, Mark would say he was going to make the vendors pay for it. We felt like we were a team. That's probably the best word for what Mark and Martin created together—a team. More Magic Dust. MicroSolutions soon grew into a company with $20 million in revenue. Cuban sold it a few years later to CompuServe.

Next, he registered domains. He would purchase an 800 number in advance of companies and industries that he knew would later want it in the future. Once again a visionary. His net worth was about $350 million when he founded AudioNet, an online streaming audio service that later became Broadcast.com, which he and his partner, Todd Wagner, sold to Yahoo for about $5.7 billion. Todd and Mark each pocketed more than $2 billion.

Mark next purchased the Dallas Mavericks, a move that was part of a carefully planned and executed path to "overnight" success. Remember, this was a guy who went from sleeping on an apartment floor to becoming a major role model of success. He had Magic Dust— and plenty of it.

That teamwork I felt at MicroSolutions carried through to me in a lot of other ways. I felt positive about everybody there. I never felt the need to go looking for another job. Instead, a company out of Portland, Oregon, that sold optical character readers recruited me to be a regional sales rep. I took that opportunity not because I wasn't happy but because it was a big salary and afforded opportunity for travel. Still, I took a lot of good experience and excellent lessons with me when I left MicroSolutions.

As I mentioned earlier, the way we went about differentiating ourselves from the market set MicroSolutions apart from everyone else. We were knocking on doors and telling people, "Hey, we do local area networks," and quite frequently the response was, "Well . . . tell us what a local area network is." After we did that, we prepared ourselves for the objections. Mark and Tony and Sally were creative when it came to that topic.

I'll never forget the most common and toughest objection—or how we responded to it: "We're really happy with our current vendors."

How would you respond if a potential client told you they were really happy with the people they worked with now?

I remember discussing with the team how we could overcome an objection from someone who was making positive comments about our competitors. Here's the reply we came up with: "Great! I'm glad you say such positive things about your current vendors. I look forward to the day when we become your vendor and you say the same things about us."

As silly as that might sound, I never forgot it. You overcome a positive with another positive.

The potential client's response was usually something like, "Hey, we'll give you a shot during the next purchase round we have." And they did that because we didn't try to compete by price or through bad-mouthing.

That's the kind of magic that happened at MicroSolutions. Ultimately, we were a team. Even though the environment was competitive, people still rooted for each other.

It was four years later that I realized I was more interested in healthcare. I liked everything I was learning about it, and I was offered the opportunity to begin in outpatient surgery centers. This led me to meet a visionary whose rise, fall, and second rise are especially inspirational, as you'll see in the next chapter.

2

Paul Herchman

Medical Alliance

"Execution is everything."

Before I tell you about Paul, I want to paint a picture for you of what healthcare was like at the time and how quickly it changed. In the late 1980s and early 1990s, the shift to transition more procedures from the inpatient hospital setting to an outpatient setting was building momentum. Paul recognized the significance of this shift and started Medical Alliance. He quickly identified procedures with minimal invasive risk and worked closely with physicians to develop protocols to perform timely procedures in an outpatient setting.

Paul came from a very entrepreneurial family.

"At seven, I was either selling Christmas cards, mowing yards, or making my neighbors buy something from me," he said. "I didn't understand the definition of entrepreneurism until I got through college. That's when I got to understand myself a little better."

From Patient to Outpatient

Paul's first job was in medical sales, selling birth control pills. At that time, if a woman had an abnormal pap, the gynecologist performed a procedure called a cold knife conization or used a CO_2 laser to remove the tissue from the cervix.

"I was trying to sell them a new portable laser," Paul said. "It was about $50,000. I ended up with a list [of doctors] who said they wanted to do the procedure in their office, but there was no way they would write me a check for $50,000. It occurred to me that if we could get the technology in their offices on a temporary basis, it would allow them to perform those procedures. That was the idea of 1989."

Paul told his friend, Kevin O'Brien, about his idea to offer state-of-the-art medical technologies to physicians *as needed*, which would allow practitioners to perform more procedures in their office. Kevin quit his job to join Paul in pursuing this idea, and they were off.

Their company, Medical Alliance, offered obvious benefits to physicians, patients, and insurance providers. Physicians spent at least 50 percent less time on a procedure because the doctor did not have to drive to the hospital to pre-op patients, then complete the procedure, and then wait still longer as the patient recovered. In the outpatient setting, a doctor could even designate a procedure room that would be more convenient for the doctor and more comfortable for the patient.

"There was momentum to see if we could transition more procedures out of surgery centers and into the offices," Paul explained. "Technology was changing very quickly. When the technology comes out, people are wary of risking their own capital. We bring those new technologies to physicians and train them, and they can offer them very quickly."

Patients were more relaxed going into an outpatient setting, knowing they were going home shortly after their procedure—rather than spending hours in a hospital environment or in a standalone outpatient surgery center. This was a simple concept with so many advantages, but it took capital to buy equipment and train staff. They also had to build confidence within the physician community to support this transition from inpatient to outpatient setting.

Nail It, Scale It

Insurance companies are always interested in lowering costs to deliver healthcare while maintaining quality, and Medical Alliance ensured both savings and quality of care. This company grew quickly and had expanded to several states by the time Paul sold it. A natural and charismatic leader, Paul surrounded himself with good players in his organization. Those were exciting times, and working side by side with physicians in those procedures helped my confidence in future relationships with the hundreds of physicians I would meet in my next adventure into specialty hospital settings.

Paul always showed compassion for the patients' side of the entire process. He was truly a visionary when it came to his concept and its outcome for the patients.

"We were building the nation's largest mobile surgical services and aesthetic laser company, and we took it public in 1996 when I was forty or so," Paul told me. "Quite a great experience, building businesses. 'Nail it, scale it,' we call it . . .

"Execution is everything if you have a business concept," Paul said. "First comes conceiving an idea, and everyone can raise their hand and say, 'Hey, I have an idea.' Then, next, you need someone to execute a plan, and for me, the most difficult thing to do is in the implementation stage."

All was not smooth sailing for Paul, as he alludes to above. When I interviewed him for this book, he shared experiences with me that would test anyone's faith. He had joined MedSurge Advances in 2003. He and his partner had major disagreements, and he was unsuccessful in completing a private equity transaction to bring in more accountability. He left the company and was soon in a proxy fight and a major legal battle. He had no income at the time. When the recession of 2008 hit, Paul—who had been so successful at starting businesses—could not get a business to work. His family struggled, and they lost the kids' college fund, their savings, and their automobiles. His wife, Donna, took a job selling men's custom clothing. On the weekends, she would sell bread at local festivals. The couple discussed whether they should stay married.

Paul is a man of faith. Even when well-meaning friends suggested he give up on big plans and just get a job, he believed there was a plan for something more in the works for him. Furthermore, he knew the only way he could pay back the money he'd borrowed from friends was if he kept seeking out opportunities.

Then he contracted an infection and was in and out of the hospital for months. One of his daily visitors was his old partner, Kevin O'Brien.

"At the end of 2011, Kevin told me he'd been praying and felt he was supposed to be working with me," Paul related. Kevin knew about a new technology that could be a beneficial and disruptive innovation in plastic surgery. The technology, Thermi, provided dermatologists and plastic surgeons with devices that applied specific amounts of heat (as opposed to generalized low, medium, or high heat) to their patients' bodies. With Thermi's products, they could apply exactly how much heat was needed to stop the flow of blood to prevent a rupture to a nerve. Once physicians saw the technology in action, they were willing to invest in it. Initially, approximately fifty physicians collectively invested more than $2 million in the company.

By February of 2016, Paul and Kevin had sold their company for $83 million. At that time, they had more than fifty physician investors and two hundred option holders to whom they distributed the money. Their first investors made up to eight times their money. Paul's prayers had been answered.

"Before, everything I touched was like gold," he said. "Then I went through this dry spell. I learned to be faithful."

Paul says he is more talented on the strategic side of the business.

"I realize I'm woefully weak in many areas of skill to make something successful. I felt from day one that I was quick to find people who were talented in the areas I was not."

Paul embodies many qualities of a visionary as I see it. He is a solution-oriented facilitator and decision maker. He is focused and persistent. Above all, he knows how to have faith in himself. Paul's talent has secured many people's financial futures, such as that of his own family—proudly including his loving wife, Donna, who never left his side. His journey to success is clearly one that has been personal, spiritual, and deeply life changing.

Mark Harris

Maxim Management Group

"Make it happen!"

As I've already told you, I started my working career as a ten-year-old paperboy delivering newspapers in the chill of the mornings in Cedar Rapids, Iowa. I always had a passion and a talent for sports, and I was inspired by the direction of my elementary school PE teacher, Hal Garwood, whom you'll read about in part III of this book. Hal was an exciting teacher and mentor, and he kept me motivated.

Back then, my high school sports included football, basketball, and baseball. Sophomore year provided an opportunity to prove myself alongside other athletes feeding into Thomas Jefferson High School, a school rich in winning tradition. I started in football and then suffered a collapsed lung, which was a huge blow to me, but it didn't stop me from playing basketball and baseball. I actually had a pretty amazing baseball season, hitting .500 as a sophomore.

Yet my parents were still telling me, "Sports won't get you a college education." So, by the time senior year rolled around, I also excelled in academics. I became a National Honor Society member while maintaining a busy athletic schedule. After playing football my senior year, I had an opportunity to play college football and signed a National Letter of Intent.

During my freshman year at Simpson College, I played both safety positions. In the second-to-last game of the season, I took a big hit on a goal-line play. The running back put his helmet directly into my chest and took us both down. Fortunately, no touchdown was made on the play, but my day was over. I lay there, gasping for air. After the game, I went to the doctor, who ordered X-rays that revealed no broken ribs or sternum. I was allowed to return to play. But two weeks later, when the season was over, I was still having difficulty catching my breath. I returned to the doctor's office, and the results from another X-ray determined I had recollapsed my lung. This time, my lung was 50 percent collapsed, and I required immediate surgery. Knowing then that my football career was over, I transferred to Coe College, which was back in my hometown of Cedar Rapids.

The following year wasn't the best. After twenty-one years of marriage, my parents divorced. I had no financial support from anybody for my entire four years of undergrad. During those college years, the true entrepreneur spirit began to bud in me. I realized I had a talent both for drumming up business and for facilitating labor to execute the work. Yes, it was facilitating that was my challenge. My grandmother was always trying to help me out with referrals for house painting and tree trimming; plus, I had painting jobs and took on even more work detasseling fields of corn. I needed help in more than one skill set. Painting is a learned skill, and walking thousands of acres to pull tassels from corn is a lot of work—not to mention you must be at least five feet six to reach up the length of the sometimes six-foot corn stalks.

I graduated in the year 1985—an event that couldn't come fast enough. After graduation, I made my way to Dallas, where I started my career in computers and electronics. As you've just read, one of my first employers was MicroSolutions, where I gravitated toward the style and vision of Mark Cuban. The environment was just what I needed to excel: there was less supervision, an opportunity to prove results, the niche allure of LAN, and a team of strong players all dedicated and motivated for success. Let me add that Cuban was full of differentiating ideas and applications to gain customers' attention. I was fortunate to be with them when the LAN technology was gaining momentum, and I was able to act fast enough to achieve a foothold in some large organizations with a higher volume of needs. After four successful years in technology, I saw an opportunity to make a change.

From Technology to Healthcare

A friend of mine had been telling me about his father's job in sales for orthopedic joint replacements. I had the opportunity to observe a couple of procedures. The father said he knew of a new opportunity in outpatient procedures that would be a great foot in the door if I wanted to enter the healthcare field. He helped set up an interview for me with Paul Herchman, and before I knew it, I was hired.

After three years with Paul and his company, I received a phone call from a recruiter by the name of Bill Vick. He told me he'd gotten my name from a highly regarded friend of mine and invited me to lunch. I went. Bill said to me, "I'm a recruiter. I got your name—I won't tell you how or where, but you're well liked in healthcare, and some of the physicians and people I talk to all the time gave me your name. I've got a company that's in the hospital business that would like to talk to you and look at your resume."

I said OK and sent him my resume. The next thing I knew, I had an interview with Continental Medical Systems in the hospital arena. They offered me an administrative position and asked if I was going to get my master's in health. I said yes, even though I had recently learned of my LSAT results and had been busy applying to law schools. Once I was in the surgery center, I realized that to transition to hospital administration would require a master's. I made a quick pivot and found an eighteen-month master of science in health administration program I could attend Friday evening, all day Saturday, and a half day on Sunday, continuing to work as I studied.

My new role was at a hospital in Alexandria, Louisiana. They called the position the COO; I was the chief operating officer and marketing director all in one. I would be working for the CEO, who told me he was going to be moving back to Oklahoma and that I would get his job in the next six months.

"Sure," I told him. "Let's do it." I went to Alexandria because I thought it gave me the best opportunity to become a CEO. There was just one little problem, which I didn't learn about until I was already there. I walked into work on day one only to learn that nine other people had already resigned.

"Boy, are you a fool for moving to Louisiana and taking this job," one of them told me on the way out.

The two doctors who were there told the staff in a meeting that the hospital was going to shut down in ten days. Although there were forty-nine beds, there were only seventeen patients in the hospital. "They are all going to be discharged in the next ten days, and you all are going to lose your jobs," the two doctors said.

They left the hospital and went across town to their nice little office. Meanwhile I called the corporate office and said, "Hey, what's going on?"

"Oh, yeah," they told me. "These guys resigned ninety days ago. It took us that long to find you and a new medical director."

It was like a sucker punch. I had come all the way from Dallas. Now I was there, and I didn't have a whole lot of options.

The next morning, I was walking down the hallway when this man with a thin frame and a lab coat past his knees came up to me. He said, "Hello, my name is Vasudeva Dhulipala. I am the new medical director. You must be Mark."

We shook hands, and I said to myself, *Oh my God, we really are going to shut down in ten days, as this guy is not from here either.* Two guys with no connections to anybody in this town are going to somehow turn this bad situation around?

Thirty days later, we had forty-one out of the forty-nine beds occupied. We continued to maintain a census average of more than 81 percent over the next eighteen months. We were recognized as the "turnaround hospital of the year" and had jumped from $9 million to $18 million in revenue.

We did it by going out to referral sources and knocking on doors. I would introduce myself directly to doctors and ask them to give us a try. We also hired a couple terrific nurse liaisons who were dedicated and excited about their roles (shoutout to Denise and Melissa). We worked hard to build a team, opened the door to as many connections in the community as we could, and simply asked for the opportunity to treat the patients who required our services. This combination brought in the patients. And twenty-five years later, Dr. Dhulipala is still there.

I'll never forget the time we had 113 referrals and more than eighty admissions in one month. The company's executives were just freaking out. They even brought in their independent outside legal counsel to interview me. They wanted to know what I was doing and saying to all these people who were sending us patients.

"What are you talking about?" I said. "I just go and talk to them and say, 'Hey, give us a try.'"

When I spoke to doctors, I'd tell them the hospital's other doctors—those who quit my first day—weren't there anymore and that we had a new medical director, whom I called Dr. D. A few months later, I would go back to a doctor's office, and everyone would say, "Hey, Dr. D's charts are very detailed, and all the patients like him and say he's really nice."

And that was it. Both Dr. D and I were in the same situation when we showed up, and I wasn't the only one who turned things around. Obviously, he got off on the right foot, and he was well liked too. One of the local physicians, Dr. Miguel Garcia, was a big supporter of the hospital while I was affiliated and worked well with Dr. D on program development.

Sometimes, I'd bring Dr. D out with me to visit other physicians one on one. He'd always say, "Hey, Mark, this is so much fun. You make it so enjoyable." Dr. D had a great bedside manner that made people comfortable with him regardless of the situation. He generously shared a few of his trust-building techniques—which obviously made our patients enjoy his care—with me and my team of nurse liaisons.

We went from $9 million to $17 million in revenue within the first year. In the second year, we opened up an outpatient clinic and added another million to make it $18 million in revenue. After that, it was time for a new challenge. I moved to a brand-new, yet-to-open twenty-one-bed inpatient physical rehabilitation hospital in Opelousas, Louisiana, just an hour and a half down the road. I took the position of CEO, and in just two weeks, we had all twenty-one beds occupied and fully staffed. I took this success as proof that it was time to venture out on my own. I started my own management company focused on inpatient physical rehabilitation hospitals, both freestanding independent facilities and hospital-within-hospital types. That's when it really all began.

All of a sudden, I was approached by the CEO of a small hospital in Eunice, Louisiana. He wanted me to open a hospital-within-hospital physical rehab facility in one wing. Then a physical therapy practice run by two therapists invited me to consult with them. Next, the doctor who had recruited me to the Opelousas physical rehab hospital contracted with me to help him grow his practice. Shortly after these three streams of income started, I found another opportunity in direct patient care. This was in the outpatient setting referred to as an ORF (outpatient rehabilitation facility), which focused primarily on the geriatric population. I opened up one clinic and grew to six clinics within a year, with revenue exceeding $2 million. Over the next three years, we went from one inpatient physical rehabilitation hospital to six hospitals. Demand for my skill set exploded in growth. By the time I was thirty-three, I had made more than $1 million net. By the time I was thirty-five, I had more than $2 million net. It was crazy for me to comprehend how this paperboy from Cedar Rapids, Iowa, was now a multimillionaire at the age of thirty-five.

I never knew what the limit was going to be. Sometimes I would say to myself, "I've done enough. It's time to get out," because I was not sitting at home counting money anyway.

I also learned to remember that some things would always be out of my control. I learned this lesson in a very real way, since in my line of work, I was forced to realize that I was never going to experience anything as difficult as losing a baby. That was the most difficult challenge I ever faced. In business, I knew what I had to do. My job was to go out and get more business, and I was good at it. But when I was holding a little baby and every medical professional I dealt with was reminding me, "Just be prepared, she might not make it"—that was a feeling of utter powerlessness.

Know When to Fold

After a few of my competitors sold, I started thinking about it too. About ten years ago, when I sold the three for $20 million, I realized that I needed to just keep doing it. Once I had the first taste of that $20 million, I knew I could go back and do it again, and that's exactly what I did. I built and sold four more businesses. Next, I had the opportunity to develop six more physical rehab hospitals as a joint venture partner. This deal fell apart because the big acute care hospital sold their interest to another big acute care hospital and killed our deal. I didn't take it too hard. Instead, I told myself, "You know what? I don't need those six hospitals to make $100 million. I'll just settle for making half of it.

"Hey, let's stick around," I told Stephanie Nunez, my CFO. "Let's open one more hospital and push ourselves to $50 million." And when we reached $42 million, I said, "I'll take the forty-two and the previous twenty, and that was going to be enough in the 24-7-365 hospital business."

People have to pick a number and know when to stop, and I figured I'd picked mine. I have no regrets and am extremely grateful. For twenty-five years, I fulfilled my passion. I created more than 3,500 jobs. More than 22,000 patients were treated in the thirty-plus facilities with which I was associated. That was extremely rewarding, and I'm proud of the work we did.

The Best Thing I Ever Did

Businesses come and go, but family is forever. My proudest accomplishment—make that my five proudest accomplishments—are my five kids. I may have been growing a company with hundreds of employees and been responsible for patients' lives and millions of dollars in revenue . . . but once I was home, I was just Dad. My kids always had to ask me to explain what I did for work. My reply was, "Healthcare," or simply, "I just work like everyone else."

The most important things in our home have always been work ethic, humility, integrity, commitment, teamwork, and family values. All five kids enjoy active lifestyles and travel. They can all tell entertaining stories and are well-liked individuals in their own right. Morgan, Zoe, Abbie, Tanner, and Sophie will all one day tell their own stories of growing up, but from my perspective, I am just a dad who couldn't have asked for better kids to raise.

One of the benefits of all those years of working was meeting many of the people I'm going to introduce you to in this book. These are people who inspired me with their Magic Dust. For years, I've known I wanted to write about, speak about, maybe even lecture about Magic Dust. Now I finally have the time and the passion to do that.

As you continue to read about the special people in this book, you will see key words that describe the qualities of Magic Dust. For the visionaries, those words include: leader, driven, persistent, determination, facilitator, team builder, committed, dedicated, strategist, and charismatic.

Let me introduce you to the implementors next, because without them, very little in business and in life would get done.

Part II
IMPLEMENTORS

Implementors are the task-oriented, multitalented, get-it-done people. They are not limited to simple one-dimensional positions. They are recognized with reverence by fellow employees, but they can also be like attack dogs when the situation calls for it. They love the idea of overcoming challenges, and they are the personification of diligence. They prepare. They plan. They research. And they are often methodical; they can plot their way to getting things done right and then recheck everything down to the last detail. These are people I personally depended on as senior management in my own company for twenty-five years, as well as others I personally have known and observed in their professional careers.

Stephanie Nunez

Maxim Management Group

"When you love what you do and who
you're doing it for, it's not work."

Stephanie Nunez is a wonderful example of an implementor and an innovator. She is a well-educated professional with an MBA degree and CPA certification. Officially the CFO for Maxim Management Group, she was also a temporary CEO at hospitals in transition at times, and she was acting COO for years once I realized she could perform both CFO/COO duties.

Stephanie is a perfectionist. Prior to hiring her, when I was inquiring about her competency from her fellow accounting colleagues, one of them told me he'd attended a continuing education course where she was present. He said that Stephanie raised her hand to correct a number calculation on a slideshow presentation, and after reviewing the error, the presenter thanked her for pointing it out.

Implementors are not looking for a fan club; they focus on getting things done and have less time for the proverbial "watercooler conversation." Stephanie was instrumental in legal and regulatory matters. She relied on Chris Johnston in Louisiana and Jonathan Henderson in Dallas for the majority of our healthcare legal and regulatory issues. Though she kept them both on speed dial, her conversations with them were usually direct and to the point. When we started building our own inpatient physical rehabilitation hospital, she was studious and always willing to learn more about construction. She was also dedicated and loyal to those she called her "peeps." She would plan her personal time far in advance so her absence wouldn't affect any ongoing projects. An incredible multitasker, she was efficient with her time. When she spent extra time to ensure everything met her standard, it was well worth it, as she was rarely wrong in her calculations.

Stephanie was my right hand. Her loyalty and commitment to the success of Maxim included selling several facilities over her twelve years and generating in excess of $60 million in sales proceeds for Maxim facilities.

Stephanie's Story

By Stephanie Nunez

When my three siblings and I were growing up, my parents instilled the importance of school and education in us. I was raised in a very small town in southwestern Louisiana. My family was not rich by any means, but we were extremely close. I had two brothers and one sister. My older brother died at thirty-five. We carried on; having a tight family helped.

When I started high school, my parents got divorced—but again, we were and are a close family. Everybody continued to get along fine, which was great for us kids. My mom is one of the best people I know.

She now lives two houses down from my dad and his current wife. My values were formed early: school, hard work, and familial love.

When I was a junior in high school, I had an opportunity to work at the local hospital while still attending school. I started from the ground up, working as a file clerk. I developed X-ray skills and just kept on learning. I wouldn't change a thing. That variety of experience has helped me over the years.

One day, while working at the hospital and still attending high school, I was in the CEO's office. He was trying to talk me into going into nursing.

"Say, sis," he said. "What you want to do after high school?"

"I want your job," I told him, not at all aware that I might have sounded bigheaded. "I want to be the CEO of a hospital."

"I believe you," he said, "and I can see you doing that."

I did have another love—basketball. And I was pretty good at it. I started in the eighth grade, but by the time I got to tenth grade, my doctor wouldn't sign my physical because of a health condition. My world was over, shattered. After that, I really put everything I had into my education.

I was driven by my focus on school and—just as importantly—my need for independence. I wanted to be able to support myself and not have to depend on other people. In 1989, I graduated from high school as salutatorian. I worked at the hospital and moved into full time while also going to college full time, which was a little challenging. I lived about an hour away from the university, so I didn't have just two full time jobs but also a long drive both ways. Looking back, sometimes I don't even know how I did it. Thanks in large part to grants and scholarships, I was able to earn a degree in accounting and finance. That taught me that education is within reach of everyone. I don't care who you are or where you came from; if you want a college education, where there's a will, there's a way.

At first, I did consider a career in nursing, but I decided it wasn't a fit for me since I'd rather be in pain myself than watch someone else suffer. I always liked math, and I also liked the business aspect of the hospital world. After graduation, I decided I needed some true accounting experience, so the administrator at my hospital opened the door for me to be hired as an accountant at an acute care hospital in Crowley. While I was there, I got my Certified Public Account license. I then worked in Lafayette as a comptroller at a rehabilitation hospital. The hospital was owned by a couple, so I was never going to be the CFO, but I liked the job and enjoyed what I was doing.

While I was working in Crowley, I decided I needed something constructive to do with my time. The University of Louisiana in Lafayette offered an MBA with a healthcare certification, so I enrolled in that program and completed it at night.

I had heard of Mark Harris and knew he had both inpatient and outpatient physical rehabilitation entities as part of his company. When his in-house legal counsel called me about a job opening for a CFO, I pretty much blew him off. I wasn't looking for a job. But then, one day, I got a phone call from Mark Harris himself.

I was perfectly content where I was. I hadn't even updated my resume. I'd blown off his attorney's call twice. But then Mark called me, and I said, "OK, I'll meet you for an interview." That is part of Mark's Magic Dust.

I've been in healthcare since I was sixteen. It's a small world, and I know people, so I started asking around about this opportunity. Everything I heard was good. So, I went for the interview, and I decided, *I'm going to give this a shot.*

I started in 2007. Mark had just bought a hospital, and I just kind of jumped in. Getting everything together and straightened out took a little while. We reopened a couple of facilities and got licenses. Mark's business was growing at the same time. There was a lot to do, with a lot of good experiences I hadn't been part of until that time. I hadn't been there that long, yet he had already given me the opportunity to be a CFO, something I'd never been before. He also needed an internal CEO for another facility in Mississippi, so I went there and did that for a while.

I like doing different things and getting a chance to show what I can do, and I definitely had that with Maxim. Mark lets people do what they're good at. I totally enjoyed working with someone who gave me a chance and had faith that I could accomplish things that even I didn't know I could. I'd never been a CEO before, but I sure did it, and I've done it multiple times since. I'm not a person who likes monotony. Working for Mark and Maxim was probably the best twelve years of my life.

In 2008, about a year after I started working for him, Mark came to me and said, "Hey, I've lived in Dallas before, and I'm kind of thinking about moving the office there. What do you think about that?"

I had a house I'd built in 2002, and I was only an hour's drive from my family.

"I'll have to think about it," I told him.

But then I thought, *Why not?* It's just a one-hour flight, and I was driving an hour to see my family anyway. My dog and I moved at the beginning of 2009. But I wasn't the only one—and here's something I think is telling. When we moved the office, the receptionist, the biller, and the plant ops guy moved with us. They did that—they moved their families—because they were working for Mark Harris, and they wanted to keep working for him.

Maxim was in the middle of operating and managing nine different facilities when I started, but when Mark made the decision to move to Dallas, he also decided to focus only on inpatient physical rehabilitation hospitals. I totally enjoyed physical rehab, since more than 80 percent of the patient population discharged home would be living independently. Dallas was the perfect place, and it offered us many opportunities. Mark had experience in behavioral hospitals and long-term acute care hospitals (LTACHs). He also preferred inpatient physical rehabilitation hospitals and stuck to owning and operating just these for almost the entire twelve years I was working with him.

Once in Dallas, Mark and I had numerous meetings as we prepared to sell the psych hospitals in Houston, Baton Rouge, and Longview. Again, he made me part of the entire due diligence process. I got to meet and learn how to interact with a variety of people. Seller and buyer are totally distinct roles, and I was thankful to be involved in both sides of the process on more than one occasion.

Every now and again, someone would ask me, "Why do you work all the time?"

I told them—and I truly believe—that when you absolutely love what you do and who you're doing it for, it's not work.

I've always enjoyed working for smaller companies because you do so many different things. That's what was happening in Dallas. One of our hospitals had a budget of $10 million—and somebody was giving me that responsibility. I watched that budget more carefully, probably, than I watched my own.

We sold the psychiatric hospitals and concentrated on rehabs. I negotiated an entire transaction in which we acquired a facility, then sold the same facility ten years later. Granted, I discussed everything with Mark, but he let me do it from start to finish. We were also building a new hospital from the ground up with a budget of more than $6 million just to build. He trusted me to manage this day to day along with the construction company.

I took care of problems, and I made decisions, right or wrong, that had to be made. But as they say, a decision is better than no decision. Mark was a levelheaded executive who was cool under pressure. If he played poker, he would easily keep a straight face.

We sold seven different hospitals for more than $60 million over the years. I say "we" because even though it's Mark's company, I've always felt that committed. Of his staff, Mark has always said, "We work together," not, "They work for me." It's always been "we" with Mark J. Harris.

Mark taught me a lot, and much of what he taught me was by example. For example, before a meeting with someone, do your homework. When I met Doug Dawson for the first time, I already knew where he worked and about his athletic successes. Mark taught me to do that research.

There is no one who knows more about the rehabilitation business than Mark Harris, and I'm not saying that only because I worked for him. He does his research. He even subscribed to the local newspapers in each area where we had a facility so he would know what was going on. That was such a valuable practice for me to learn. He also read several healthcare publications weekly, and his memory was something I stopped questioning. After second-guessing him for the first five years, I said to myself, *He doesn't guess, so it must be right.*

One of Mark's Magic Dust qualities is giving people the opportunity to take something they're good at and do it. Whenever we were looking at a new goal, one of his favorite expressions was, "Make it happen." That motivates me to this day.

I believe in getting the job done. No matter what it is or where it is, you do what you have to do. If I go to a hospital and I see trash anywhere, I pick it up. If I expect an employee to do something, I expect myself to do it too. That's just work ethic. You do whatever you need to do. Mark's biggest pet peeve—and the quickest way to a termination—was to say, "It's not my job." His business card listed only his name, with no title and not even his master's degree. He was always willing to step in and help with any project and frequently drove all night to be at surveys for new facilities.

To me, Magic Dust is whatever really good thing someone has to bring to the table, whether in a corporate environment or in Little League, no matter what you're doing. Don't let anybody tell you that you can't do something. You can do anything you want to do if you put your mind to it. You have the Magic Dust. You're the one who has to cultivate and run with it.

Elizabeth Bennett

Corporate Clinical Officer, Maxim Management Group

"What an experience it's been."

When I think of Liz Bennett, I think of her efficiency, her natural attention to detail as a nurse in patient care, and her meticulous perfection in her documentation on patient charts. Her Magic Dust qualities include attention to detail and knowledge of the documentation required in the volumes of policy and procedures that must be maintained in JCAHO hospitals. Her continued ambition and desire for more education was encouraged at Maxim Management Group.

Liz and I worked together for sixteen years, and today she serves as a director of clinical services, with all clinical personnel reporting to her. She was a single mother of three when we met and was also the nurse who would rather cover a shift herself than call in the contract nursing company. She clearly enjoyed teaching the staff and showing them how she wanted things done.

She was also very focused on our daily, ongoing survey preparedness at each facility. The hospital industry is highly regulated, and documentation is required daily for patient care, employee staff, and administration of each facility. In the healthcare industry, the building is considered part of the environment of care, and there are several requirements that must be met, including being prepared for all weather conditions, frequent fire and health and safety drills, and other emergency-response situations. Liz always stayed current with the regulations and seemed to enjoy reviewing open and closed patient charts and mock-survey drills.

Yes, this implementor knew her details and kept our facilities in accordance with the JCAHO standards at all times in multiple states, which is no simple task. Liz was committed to pursuing her Certified Rehabilitation Nurse designation and, after years of documenting her progress, accomplished that goal.

Liz had Magic Dust in many qualities, such as leading by example in the delivery of patient care. She has never been a person comfortable behind a desk. She enjoys sharing her years of experience in patient care and her uncanny knowledge of the documentation required for continued compliance at several facilities daily. This attunement is truly Magic Dust. In her sixteen-plus years at Maxim Management Group, she moved toward her own desires for personal acknowledgment and professional advancement. She was one of the intricate players in the growth and success of Maxim. Read her story, and you'll see why.

Elizabeth's Story

By Elizabeth Bennett

When I was eight years old, I knew I wanted to be a nurse. I have always been a natural caregiver and desired to help others. When I graduated from high school, I had to choose between nursing and accounting. I choose nursing because it seemed to offer the most job opportunities. After I graduated from nursing school in 1985, I ended up working in a small hometown community hospital. It had only twenty-one beds and an emergency room. On the shifts I worked, I was the lone registered nurse, with LPNs and aides. While there, I worked the emergency room as well as the medical-surgical floors, so I gained valuable experience early on in my career.

With so few RNs, I quickly took an interest in patient documentation. After leaving there, I spent about four years working in nursing homes and was promoted to management. A new impatient physical rehabilitation hospital was being built in Leesville, Louisiana. The town was buzzing with interest when I happened to be at the doctor's office for an appointment with my husband. One of the medical staff on the soon-to-open inpatient physical rehabilitation hospital happened to be our own physician. My husband and I had just recently gotten married, and the doctor asked me about my background. When I mentioned that I was a nurse, he quickly said, "Well, we might need to talk." And then he suggested I interview.

I had experience with state surveys and attention to compliance. He recommended me to Mark. I became the first employee at the inpatient physical rehabilitation facility in Leesville, Louisiana. When I first came to work, there was still construction going on. I could smell the new floors. I had to bring a folding chair from home just to sit down. In those early days before I had my own laptop, I borrowed my husband's.

One day, Mark walked in and handed me a two-foot stack of papers. Those papers were our policies and procedures for the new facility. That was the beginning of our working relationship. We divided the responsibilities, and I realized early on that Mark was a delegator and expected me to carry my share of the policy and procedures. Mark was also a hospital administrator and had already gone through a few other opening surveys with JCAHO.

We worked nonstop getting the facility open. I started in August. We were not scheduled for a survey until November. Then the state called and said they could do one in mid-September, but it had to be done by the end of the month. We scrambled to hire a twenty-four-seven working staff and got the facility open one week before the state survey. We had worked hard to pass our first JCAHO certified facility. This was a significant accomplishment, achieved by basically just the two of us.

I left the Leesville rehab for a period of time to be a director of nursing (DON) at an acute care hospital. I received a call from Stephanie Nunez about an opportunity to return to Maxim to oversee other facilities in multiple states. It truly changed my life.

The position was available immediately, and they offered me the job. I couldn't go to work immediately, however, because I hadn't been cleared by my physician following a recent eye procedure. They kept the position open for a month, however, while I recovered. Soon after I started, we opened two facilities together for Maxim. One was in Texas.

When I was only dreaming of a nursing career, I had no idea I would end up where I have. The opportunities and the personal growth I gained while working with Maxim were a testament to the empowerment and integrity I felt there. I was given responsibility and support in making decisions; I could feel the trust the organization had in me. The positive culture created at Maxim truly made going to work extremely rewarding and gratifying. I hope I have been able to give back to the people in my departments, just as so much was given to me.

I think you're born with a little bit of Magic Dust. You have to develop it in yourself. I've learned that every individual is different. The best way to get somebody to do something that you want them to do is to lead by example. I have had to take my own advice on that sometimes, because I have had nurses call out on the day of their shift and have had to cover for them myself. Rather than stressing over a schedule, I'd say, "Forget it. I'll work it. I need to stay sharp in my skills anyway."

In thirty-four years of nursing, I've had to give only two legal depositions, and in only one of them was I the actual nurse in the situation. The extra hours spent paying attention to detail and my knowledge of JCAHO documentation have proven to be critical. If I have something unexpected come up, I ask the nurse involved, "OK, if you had to defend this decision, would you do it the same way again? Will your documentation prove that?"

I like people who are willing to learn, to step outside the box and do things that may not be exactly their responsibility to get done. I like people like me, who want to make things happen. If something needs to be done, let's just jump in there and do whatever we have to do to make it happen.

Mark told me early on, "We will wear many different hats," and we have. I admire people who keep pushing themselves to learn and do more. I encourage others to invest in themselves. Read, and ask questions. If I could offer only one piece of advice to someone younger, it would be this: Get all the basic experience you can. I gave this advice to my own daughter, who just graduated from nursing school. You get out there, and you learn the basics of med-surg or ER—every experience you can as a young nurse. Take it in before you get into a management position, and it will serve you well.

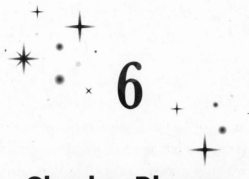

Charles Pierson

Former President and CEO of Big Brothers Big Sisters of America

"Turn a negative into motivation."

Can you run a nonprofit like a corporation? You can if you have faith and heart as well as drive and a passion for excellence. That's what Charles Pierson had and what he accomplished with Big Brothers Big Sisters of America. When he was president and CEO of the local organization, I called him and told him the story of my "little brother," Tom, and how he and I still couldn't get rid of each other after more than thirty-five years. Charles loved the story and invited me and Tom to meet him at the Big Brothers Big Sisters office in Irving, Texas.

When Tom and I arrived for the meeting, I could tell Tom was nervous. He told me how much he was looking forward to meeting the CEO of the program. Once inside the lobby, we noticed plaques and pictures of other celebrity-status individuals who had supported the mission of Big Brothers Big Sisters. Tom said, "I never realized that this was such a big-deal organization, with fancy offices and a real business environment."

I reminded him that during my call with Charles Pierson, I had been able to sense that Charles understood the value of our long-term relationship, as shown by his quick invitation to meet us at the company offices. Charles met us with a huge smile and welcoming handshakes; his hand was like a large mitten compared to our normal-sized hands. He watched how Tom and I interacted and was interested in our earlier years, back when we were first matched. He was curious about how we'd managed to stay connected for what I now know is going to be a forever relationship.

Charles asked Tom genuine and direct questions about growing up and about how our match grew into a friendship and mentoring relationship. Tom commented a couple times that Charles must have played football, given his overall frame and thick neck, shoulders, and torso. Charles was six feet two and a 260-pound block of muscle, still young at fifty-seven years.

During our meeting, Charles pointed out several framed pictures in cases along the walls. He impressed on us that many of today's successful leaders started out as "Littles" in the program themselves. Tim Brown was a Little who later went on to play football at Notre Dame, won the Heisman Trophy, and played a Hall of Fame career in the NFL. Charles complimented Tim Brown's commitment to the program and mentioned how important it was for current and future matches to see how anybody could be a part of this awesome program.

Tom noticed a PSA video that featured former Dallas Cowboy and Hall of Fame quarterback Troy Aikman. Troy served as a public spokesman for the BBBS organization and made commercials supporting the mission of helping to match young boys and girls with positive role models.

One thing that was obvious to me was that Charles was not a mere figurehead in his role as CEO. He was all in, and his interest in my relationship with Tom was sincere. He was also active in recruiting financial supporters and building up his organization's structure and focused on matches that would increase public awareness of the program. He had a vision of future growth that he maintained for his nine years with the organization.

After our visit with Charles, he must have decided our story was solid, because he asked us to record an interview to be played at an upcoming gala—one that was the biggest annual fundraiser the program had in Dallas. Charles was a master at bringing in local celebrities to attend the gala, including players from the Dallas Cowboys and the Dallas Mavericks—the likes of Jason Terry and Dirk Nowitski, the Hall of Fame star who led the Mavericks to their first and only NBA championship title. Mike Modano and Jamie Benn of the Dallas Stars have also helped promote BBBS at public events, such as the NHL draft.

Tom and I recorded the video and attended the 2013 gala, which featured a performance from country-western superstar Trace Adkins and special guest T. Boone Pickens, who was a board member and longtime supporter of BBBS. While at the gala that night, Tom and I had the privilege of hosting Mr. and Mrs. Darvis "Doc" Patton at our table for the evening. Darvis is a two-time Olympic silver medalist. The list of supporters could go on. I trust this mention will continue to bring awareness to this great community-based program.

When Charles decided to accept the role as CEO of BBBS National, he moved temporarily to Philadelphia, where the original national office was. During his term, he traveled to the Fiesta Bowl in Phoenix, which was sponsored by Frito-Lay on a national level. I was also in Phoenix for the game and enjoyed spending time with Charles and his wife, Pam, at a few of the first-class events sponsored by Frito-Lay. I also had a personal interest in the bowl game itself since my daughter Morgan was attending Oklahoma State University, who was playing Stanford University, led by future NFL star Andrew Luck as their quarterback. The game was one of the most dramatic and fun games to watch, with plenty of scoring for both teams. The game was suspenseful all the way to the last minute. It even went into overtime before the Weeden-led OSU Cowboys pulled out a 41–38 victory. The national Big Brothers Big Sisters award was given at this game as well. This further showed the instrumental effort Charles had made in working with incredible civic-minded people like Al Gordon—a VP at the Frito-Lay corporate office in Plano, Texas, whom we were fortunate to have as a board member of Big Brothers Big Sisters—and corporations like Frito-Lay that understand the value of giving back to their communities nationwide. I am proud to have a brotherly relationship with Charles Pierson. We are both former football players who have used our interests and passions to help others. Thank you again to Charles for his above-and-beyond contributions, which have made a lasting impact on thousands of people. His Magic Dust is obvious.

Keep reading to learn more about Charles. First, though, I want to share a story few know about him, T. Boone Pickens, and Trace Adkins, all generous people who united for a cause.

The Fundraiser

One night in early 2013, I was watching an episode of *The Apprentice* in which country singer Trace Adkins appeared as a contestant and had a challenge to raise money for a cause. While he was sitting in an empty deli in New York City, making phone calls for donations, a young lady walked in and presented him with a check. I was especially interested since I recognized her outfit at once. I knew the bright orange colors the young woman was wearing; they represented OSU, my daughter Morgan's college in Stillwater, Oklahoma.

The young woman handed Trace an envelope. When he opened it, he was overcome. It was a check for $35,000 from none other than T. Boone Pickens, the business magnate and oil wildcatter—and, it just so happened, a member of our national BBBS board.

"I've never met Mr. T. Boone Pickens," Trace Adkins said as he held that check. "But if there's anything I can ever do for you, I'd be glad to do it."

I called Charles Pierson right away and said, "You've got to call T. Boone and get him to ask Trace Adkins to come sing at our gala in the fall."

That's exactly what happened. Not only did he sing, he donated his fee to BBBS and also helped raise more donations by taking pictures with patrons at the gala. I was at the gala that night and enjoyed hearing Trace sing. T. Boone even flew in for the event—and, of course, to meet Trace. Watching the two of them sitting on bar stools on the stage together—Trace is about six feet seven, T. Boone about a foot shorter—is one of my favorite BBBS memories. Both men were so gracious in their support of each other's philanthropic activities. Shoutout to Trace Adkins for an incredible performance that night.

Now, let's let Charles tell his story.

Charles's Story

By Charles Pierson

I grew up as a military dependent. My father was a lieutenant in the army for twenty-one years, and his father was killed in World War II. My father's twin brother was also killed in a plane crash when he was trying to go to Vietnam, where my dad was stationed. As you can imagine, we were and are big believers in military service.

My grandmother was an incredible woman—a teacher who overcame cancer and who lost her husband when my dad and his twin brother were three years old. Although she ultimately remarried, she raised them alone. Then, as I said, she lost one of her twin sons in that plane crash. My mom's dad, my granddad, pretty much raised me while my mom was getting a college education. My family was grounded in Christian faith—something that became personal for me when I was a teenager—and I credit my grandmother and the rest of my family for those values, which I still live by today.

I was taught to believe in God and family. When I met and fell in love with my wife, I knew I wanted to marry her even though I was eighteen and she was nineteen at the time. If you're the son of a military man, what do you do? You apply to military academies—West Point, the Air Force Academy—and that's what I did. It's a pretty long process, and I was about halfway through it when I realized I'd already served eighteen years. I was born in Italy, moved to Germany, and attended eleven different schools between my kindergarten and senior years.

In that situation, you were either strong at the core as a family or you were weak at the core as a family, which was a recipe for disaster, one that usually included drugs and alcohol. Fortunately, because of our faith and our solid foundation, I—with a loving mom and dad and a fantastic older sister—was OK. But I also felt bound to our family's tradition.

I went to my dad and said, "Are you going to be disappointed in me if I don't apply for the academy?"

"No," he said. "Why would you think that?"

Just like that, my dad removed the expectation from my shoulders.

My goals back then were pretty uncomplicated. I really just wanted to go to college and play football. However, I was only six feet and two and a half inches (which I rounded up to six-three!) and 235 pounds out of high school, and I wasn't highly recruited by everybody in the country to play for them. This was 1981, and the Division I schools were looking for players a minimum of six-four and 250 pounds or heavier. "We think you're a good player," they told me. I was just a little bit undersized.

That didn't crush my dream. I'd already dealt with doubt. In my sophomore year of high school, I'd told my coach that my dream was to play college football.

He looked at me and laughed. "You're not big enough to play college football," he said.

I think he honestly believed it. But he was mistaken about a few things. First, I was a sophomore, so I still had opportunity to grow. Second, and most importantly, he was measuring my size. He wasn't measuring my heart.

I went to Vanderbilt University. After a redshirt year, I played the next four on a football scholarship. So many times in college football when I was going up against a bigger guy, I was excited because I knew I could outhustle and outsmart him if I worked hard.

There's a difference between potential talent and realized talent.

You can't believe what someone tells you about your potential. Take that negativity the way I took what that high school coach told me: turn it into motivation and determination. Ultimately, you'll be judged by your realized talent, not by someone else's opinion of you.

That motivation has played a big part in my life. I'll tell you about a coach who used it in a positive way. We were playing in the regional finals. I was going up against an all-state lineman. Coach Dickerson, who had a major effect on me and was a big influence in my life, happened to be outside the locker room.

"Chuck," he said, "that kid you're playing against this week is pretty good."

"Coach, are you saying he's better than I am?" I asked.

He just shrugged. I knew he was doing it to motivate me, and I made sure out there on the field that he didn't question who the greater player was.

I earned a bachelor's degree in finance and marketing and a master's degree in business administration. My wife was a nurse and worked for two years while I was finishing school. Obviously, money was tight, so we agreed to go in and unlock our church in exchange for free rent while we lived in the church basement. Not many people knew there was an apartment in the basement of the church, so if we didn't lock the door, we had people walking in. After school, we moved to Birmingham, and I cut my teeth with a natural gas company.

I was neon green. I didn't know anything. I had a great textbook education and great theoretical work, but I had not yet had to apply that to the real world. I managed to secure a job as an accountant for a manufacturer of rubber components. When I had the opportunity to apply for a position in Mexico, I had little expectation of getting it. When I did, my wife, Pam, was so supportive and encouraged the move to Mexico with no hesitation. This was my shot at putting my skills and talents to the test—and, in the process, trying to learn Spanish. This was a project manager position; the next step was general manager, which I had set my sights on achieving. As fate would provide, there was an open position for a general manager position in Dallas, Texas, and I was ecstatic when I was chosen for the position three years later.

Big Brothers Big Sisters

I had always believed in the work of Big Brothers Big Sisters, and I felt called to go to work for them. I became president and CEO of North Texas Big Brothers Big Sisters. When I was hired, they were merging three chapters together. After that, we were the third largest of the 350 groups across the country. In ten years, we became the largest in the country. Not only did we go to the number-one spot, we were twice the size of the second largest. We were doing things that no other agency had ever done. We had an incredible staff and an amazing mission. That experience has been a great source of joy for me.

Furthermore, we grew the matches we made from 3,406 to more than 10,000; we tripled the budget; and we went from 90 employees to 225. Everything went so well there that they asked me to become national president and CEO.

Role Models

When I think of role models, I don't have to look far. Some people are born with that Magic Dust quality of determination, but it can be learned. Football taught me. When you play football, you're going to get knocked down and get dirty, and you have to decide if you're going to give up or keep trying.

I had many role models in football, but probably the greatest role model I've ever known was my grandmother. When I was in college, my wife and I loved to go to her house. She always fed us well, and although she didn't have a lot of money, she always gave us some. One day, I noticed that her big, heavy freezer was in a different part of the house.

"Granny," I asked, "how did that freezer get moved?"

"I moved it."

"By yourself?" I asked.

"Yes."

"Granny, I'm forty-five minutes away. Why didn't you wait until I got here?"

"Because it had to be moved."

She left me a great legacy and a great example. When I was in college, my dad died of brain cancer. Granny had already lost her second husband, who had been diagnosed with MS shortly after their marriage. There I was, twenty-one years old, and we had just buried my hero. Yes, I was feeling sorry for myself. We went to my grandmother's house to be together and share the food the church members had brought. It was Wednesday night. When I looked up, I saw that she had put on her coat and was standing there in it.

"Granny," I said. "What are you doing?"

"Going to go to church."

"Are you kidding me?"

I thought she'd sit around the table grieving, but her attitude was simple. It was Wednesday, and this is what we do. We go to church.

Yes, football taught me a lot, and my grandmother taught me more.

The rest of the implementors you will meet here are all about family.

Greg Bjornsen, Bjornsen Investments

Greg Bjornsen's grandfather started in construction. His son—Greg's late dad, Terry—saw the bigger picture and was a developer who hired construction companies. Originally, they did both residential and commercial work. The company evolved into commercial development only. Now, under Greg's leadership as CEO and with the leadership of his brothers Kevin and Steve, the forecast is bright. In 2019, the fourth generation, which includes Greg's son, Jake, and Steve's son, Alec, joined as well.

Long-term relationships survive when there are trustworthy and reliable landlords and tenants. Greg has a stable client base because he and his family have spent years understanding the market and the customers' needs. It's a calculated risk to build for clients with long-term tenant relationship hopes. Realizing those opportunities is what Bjornsen Investments has been fortunate to call its Magic Dust.

That same long-term commitment and dedication bodes well for the Bjornsen family in their personal lives as well. The first three generations celebrated their marriage vows by spending an average of forty years together. I would not call this luck, since the family has lived their personal lives in the same manner they have conducted their business. Long-term relationships are valued and preserved with the Magic Dust qualities of integrity, loyalty, appreciation, determination, commitment, and dedication.

Charles Terrell Jr., Terrell Insurance Services

Charlie Terrell Jr. grew up in the heyday of Dallas's high school Friday night lights football. After a solid senior year at Highland Park, a perennial state-championship winner, he decided to join the team at SMU. Charlie Jr. had a brief football stint on the team with the famous "Pony Express," which included the likes of Eric Dickerson and Craig James as the running backs, both of whom went on from SMU to NFL careers. Charles Sr. happened to have enjoyed a much longer career, which included earning Academic All-American status for the SMU Mustangs.

After graduation, Charles Sr. launched an insurance company under the name Unimark; it later became Terrell Insurance Services when Charlie Jr. returned to Dallas after spending time in Atlanta, California, and a brief opportunity with the Staubach real estate company. He enjoyed having the opportunity to be affiliated with a great leader like Roger Staubach, as well as Roger's huge following of other highly successful athletes, who worked with the same company for years.

When Charles Sr. mentioned working together, it was perfect timing for Charles Jr., who was ready to enter the insurance business and work with his father. The Magic Dust that the father-son duo enjoyed was their ease of conversation and skill at listening. So many people forget these qualities are hugely important when growing a business in a field like insurance, as many business owners are required to have insurance and there are several options in the marketplace.

The passing of Charles Sr. in 2020—during the writing of this book—was a huge loss for the Terrell family. Charlie Jr. has continued the family business and has three sons of his own who will have the opportunity to continue the business if they choose. When Charles Sr. and Charlie Jr. worked together, either of them might call you and both might attend a meeting, since both were well aware of each customer— the relationships were personal for sure. As a fellow business owner, I know that networking to build contacts for future opportunities is always important, and I appreciated both Terrells' willingness to open doors to their contacts for me. I hope they never change their method of doing business, since it's working, and that they keep sharing their Magic Dust.

Steve Knox

Lifetime Gutters and More

"Not everything works out exactly as you plan."

Steve Knox owns a roofing and gutter company, another family business, in rural northeast Iowa. He is proof there are no shortcuts when it comes to building a solid reputation, something he has also taught his son, Troy, who has worked with him from the start. Because they're in the snow belt, they don't even advertise. They shut down for five months, and Steve farms. When they open up again, they have all the work they can handle. That's what happens when you're known for focusing on quality.

Steve and I met the old-fashioned way: we were next-door neighbors when we were kids. Our parents were really close, and although Steve and I were friends throughout high school, once I went off to college we didn't see each other anymore. It wasn't until about twelve years ago that we reconnected at a wedding, and then it was as if no time had transpired. Here's Steve to tell you his story.

Steve's Story

By Steve Knox

If you ask what drives me, I'd have to say an honest day of work. A close tie would be any time spent with family. With seven grandchildren in my life, I've learned to put work on the back burner now and then. My company does general construction—any exterior work on homes. I have to be doing something. I don't mind working a lot of hours. That keeps me sane, I guess.

I got married very young, at age eighteen, and my life changed pretty quickly. It was a challenge, but it turned out to be a great situation because I have three wonderful kids: a daughter, Carrie, and two sons, Travis and Troy. Still, it's pretty strange when a senior in high school has to have his wife write him an excuse to get out of school because he has to work.

Back in 1984, I started working at a plastics manufacturing company. I worked there twenty-five years on the night shift and did construction work during the day. That was what put the bread on the table. At the factory, I teamed up with another guy who was a lot like I was in terms of work ethic. We started our construction company. It went well for a couple of years, and we decided to buy out our competition. By then, I was divorced. My business partner and I had a lot of money tied up in this company. We were working hard, and I thought we were pretty successful.

But one night, my banker knocked on my door and said, "I can't get a hold of your partner, and guess what? You are broke."

I was pretty much stuck with the business. My banker said, "I know you, and I know you can make it work."

It was very tough going. There was a lot of debt at that time. Amy, the woman who became my wife, was a big help. She has a degree in accounting and a full-time job as a supervisor at a local creamery. She was helping me out and found a lot of discrepancies in my books. When she left her full-time job, she became my full-time office manager, and that's what she's been ever since.

That tells you a lot about her. She is extremely supportive and an excellent listener. She can sort things out for people and help them see the big picture. Her ability to organize and coordinate multiple tasks has made my life much more productive and actually efficient. Amy did not have any children of her own and has become a natural grandma to the seven grandkids. We have both enjoyed sharing them with my three kids, who frequently leave them with us for their date nights and sometimes for vacations.

We've taken lots of trips with the grandkids. Amy came up with the idea of an RV vacation so that, instead of flying, we could just hang out, with the grandkids coming and going. It was perfect. I always tell her how blessed we are that we all have our health and that our kids all live so close to us. I wouldn't want it any other way.

New Venture

When my business partnership was dissolved, I ended up with a 250-foot-long building that was also my shop. One renter left, so Amy and I talked it over, and we both went to auctioneer school. It was a lot of hard work, but it was also an exciting challenge.

Finally, everything got to be too much for me to juggle, so I sold the building and the auction business to the man who had been helping me do the auctions. I told him, "This is what I want," and he wrote me a check right there.

Now we work out of our house and our new shop. The gutter business was something I grasped, since it was out of doors and I got to use my hands each day. The opportunity to work with both of my two boys at the beginning was like a dream come true, though it was short lived. My oldest son, Travis, enjoys operating heavy machinery and soon found opportunities he wanted more. Troy, my youngest son, has taken on the responsibility of co-CEO; it will not be a surprise when he one day just takes it off my hands.

We grew the business from only gutters to roofing since we were actually doing both repairs for several of our customers anyway. Troy is a better family man then I was. He has been able to manage his three kids and wife with much better balance than I did. I believe good advice is to try to maintain that balance between your job and family so you can enjoy them both more.

Farming in the Blood

I grew up on a farm. I couldn't wait to get out of school, run to my uncle's, and start chores. Farming is something I have a passion for; it is in my blood, and it is my escape. Matter of fact, I recall one summer when Mark Harris came to stay a couple weeks in our neck of the woods here in Waukon, Iowa. He actually wasn't too bad at bailing hay and using a pitchfork.

That's what I'd like to do in retirement. However, I wouldn't be able to hobby farm if I didn't have a job to support it. It's relaxing for me to sit on a tractor for four hours a day, and sometimes it's easier to talk to cows than to some people.

Life has taught me that you really need to focus on your goals, on what you want to accomplish. At the same time, don't be afraid to take a second look and go down a different path. Not everything works out exactly like you plan. If you're going to try something, give it 100 percent.

Jim Kelly

Key Account Manager

"I wanted to stay with just one employer."

When I think of Jim Kelly, I think of stability: stability in his relationships, including his marriage, his career, and his friends. We met in Dallas around 1986. Jim lived in an apartment complex called the Village, where a lot of people from out of state were living. I'm from Iowa, and Jim is from Ohio. We got to know each other a little bit from hanging out, and we decided to room together for a couple of years.

Jim grew up in a suburb of Cleveland. His dad was born and raised in Ireland and came to this country at age fourteen. He served in World War II, and he and Jim's mom had five sons. Two of their sons, Jim's brothers, went into the military. Jim, the fourth son, was the first to get a college degree, a business degree from Kent State. After school, he went to work in Cleveland as an underwriter for Aetna.

"Then they offered to transfer me to either Tampa, Denver, or Dallas," Jim said. "My brother lived in Houston, so I picked Dallas."

But Jim realized he was too active to like sitting behind a desk all day. In high school, he used to deliver office supplies, so he interviewed for an office supply company in Dallas and went to work for them. At the time I wrote this book, he had been in the office supply business thirty-four years, thirty-one of them with his current company, where he works as a key account representative.

"My dad was with his job for thirty-five years," Jim told me. "I wanted to follow that example and stay with just one employer. My goal has been to work for and retire from the same company."

It's rare to see that kind of loyalty and stability today, but that's what Jim is all about. He's also all about family. He met his wife in 1987. Jim signed up for a tennis league to meet girls, though I don't think he even played tennis at the time. He met a girl, though. Sara was also in that league. They were married in 1990. Now empty nesters, they have three daughters (Loren, Katie, Rachel), and while I was writing this book, they had just returned from a family trip to Ireland.

"We wanted to see where my dad was raised," Jim told me. "That was a bucket-list item, and it was extra special because we were with our family."

His wife had been diagnosed with breast cancer a couple of years before, but she is doing well. He has taken on that challenge as he does everything: with a positive attitude. Jim was planning his retirement based on a dollar amount he'd set as a goal. Jim said that after Sara survived her initial health battle, those plans changed. Together, they traveled to California, Hawaii, and Ireland. He said the trips wouldn't have mattered as much without the love of his life by his side.

It's no surprise that Jim admires honesty in both his personal and work lives.

"Also, when you deal with someone, it has to be two-way communication," he told me. "You listen to what I have to say, and vice versa."

He enjoys the people he does business with. "A lot of my customers are in healthcare," he explained. "They are very friendly, and I like that. It means a lot."

Jim loves travel, golf, and just about anything you can do outdoors. At age sixty, he can still sit on a boat dock with a ski rope in hand, tied to a jet ski, and go from zero to fifty in seconds. I'm here to tell you that Jim is a slalom water skier, and he looks like a twenty-something on the water.

He also believes you can develop Magic Dust qualities. He gives credit to his parents, his primary role models, for helping him shape the qualities that have made him who he is. In his dad, he saw a loyal husband, father, and employee. In his mom, he saw a nurturer. Jim and his parents always read people really well and were extremely well liked.

"My mom was a very hard worker, a stay-at-home mom while we were growing up, and she probably did more for us than most moms do today," he said. "When we went on fishing trips to Lake Erie, she'd help cook the fish, and she was known for her special desserts, like homemade M&Ms cookies, strawberry chiffon pie, and gingerbread with lemon sauce."

As retirement approaches, Jim has plans to fill that extra time. He's not exactly sure what he'll do first, but he knows that travel and golf are in his future. "I'd also like to volunteer as an usher at sporting events and for Habitat for Humanity."

What else?

"You never know," he said. "Variety is the spice of life."

As you can see, the implementor category is not one size fits all. Regardless of their career path, these people are caring and committed, remain consistent in their actions, and honor their word. They are focused and professional people, driven by loyalty you can (and likely will) take to the bank. Now we move on to a new group—those who make achieving fun, who make regular people feel like superstars, and who prove every day, by example, that you can achieve any goal. Let's meet the motivators.

Part III
MOTIVATORS

Motivators make us want to act like them. They make us want to step up our game and improve ourselves. Furthermore, they teach us to be aware of our role, and they remind us that no matter what that role is, it counts. Motivators make us appreciate just being on the team with them and make us want others to appreciate being on our team too.

The Magic Dust in motivators is special. They are people who possess skills or talents that are difficult to learn—traits such as charisma, leadership, influence, persistence, dedication, commitment, and the desire to be team players who are inspirational in their usefulness.

9

Doug Dawson

Dawson Financial Services and Former NFL Player

"Pray like it's all up to God, and work like it's all up to me."

Doug Dawson is a wonderful example of a motivator. At age fourteen, he was playing on the B team in football but making bold predictions of his future as a starting player. As a student who received two Bs in the classroom, he stated that he planned to graduate as one of the top ten students in his class. Doug didn't let these early challenges dampen his ambition to hit the gym and keep studying even harder so he could back up his predictions. After a stellar high school career, Doug played college football at the University of Texas, where he received first team all-American honors and was selected as an Outland Trophy finalist as one of the top-five linemen in the nation. He went on to play eleven years in the NFL.

He also excelled in academics and earned a degree in petroleum engineering from University of Texas. He decided to become an investment planner with Northwestern Mutual while still playing football full time. The dual commitment didn't slow Doug's persistent rise in the ranks at Northwestern Mutual. In fact, he even reached as high as top ten in a pool of more than 9,500 agents worldwide.

Doug's commitment as a father to his daughter, Arlin, and son, Ross, has always been a priority. He also makes time for causes in his community, such as the American Cancer Society in Houston, speaks often to future athletes at FCA, and is always active in church, where he shares his faith.

When Doug and I met, we immediately established mutual respect and realized we were kindred spirits with many common threads. Doug and I became lifelong friends and have been business associates since 1998. We have shared vacations and stayed at each other's homes, and our children have enjoyed watching our friendly but always competitive activities, whether it be ping-pong games, jet ski races, or just doing flips off a fourteen-foot-high boat dock. Yes, this man leads by example and has always been a natural motivator.

When you go out with Doug Dawson, he takes you to places where everybody knows him. The last time we had dinner, his already larger-than-life personality filled the whole room. He calls himself a "delusional optimist," but I don't think there's anything delusional about him. Instead, I believe Doug's many successes result from a combination of faith, drive, natural charisma, and Magic Dust. Here, in his own words, is the story of his journey.

Doug's Story

By Doug Dawson

Both my parents are from Oklahoma. My dad arrived at Rice University in Houston back in the 1950s, when education was free, to study for a career as a petroleum geologist. My mom, a fashion merchandising major, went to Oklahoma State and moved after her senior year to work as a buyer for Foley's, a chain of stores owned by May Department Stores and headquartered in Downtown Houston. They met in 1956 and married the following year. My older brother was born in 1959, and I followed in 1961. We moved to New Orleans, then to Lafayette, and then back to Texas about the time I was four or five.

Even before I could put a name to it, I had what I call "delusional optimism." First and foremost, I think it's a really strong faith in God and a belief that all things work together for good to those who love God and are called according to His purpose. The bottom line is that I have strong confidence that the final outcome is heaven.

Before I understood that concept, I had already experienced delusional optimism. I must have. When I was in the eighth grade, I went to my high school counselor. When she asked, "What's your goal?" I said, "To be in the top ten of my class."

"The top 10 percent?" she asked.

"No," I replied. "The top ten!"

"Well," she said. "What you have to do is earn all As."

I didn't take her seriously. That first year, I made two Bs in biology, which made it clear to me that I probably was not going to be a doctor. From that point forward, however, I never earned another B in high school. I graduated in the top ten—eighth out of a class of six hundred kids.

I don't know how it happened, but I was pretty much a compulsive nutjob when I was in middle school. I remember always being motivated—not by success but by fear of failure. No option; I just did what I needed to do to avoid failure. And once it happened, there was satisfaction, but then I moved on. So my highs were never too high, but my lows were never too low, which is, I think, a real positive.

When I was a freshman in high school, I wanted to attend Colorado School of Mines and get a petroleum engineering degree. I always wanted to be in the oil business like my father. Because I was good with numbers, I decided on a career as a petroleum engineer instead of one as a geologist.

When I entered my freshman year, I was five feet eight and 140 pounds, a pretty good athlete on the B team. Then I hit something called puberty, and I shot to six feet three and 240 pounds by the beginning of my senior year. At 240 pounds, I ran a five-thirty mile and was the highest ranked offensive lineman in the state, maybe in the country, so I was highly recruited. The University of Texas has a strong engineering school, and I earned the petroleum degree in four years while playing football. I was a consensus and Academic All-American. Then I was drafted by the St. Louis Football Cardinals in the second round of the 1984 draft. I had a $350,000 signing bonus and a base salary of $120,000. So, I literally had made $470,000 just by signing my name on that line.

Injury and Inspiration

The summer before my third year on the team, as a way to save some money, I had purchased an insurance policy from John Qualley, a Northwestern Mutual representative. In my third year, in 1986, I ruptured my Achilles. I went back to training camp in 1987 and partially tore it again. In August of 1987, I ended up having a third surgery on my Achilles and was told I would never again play football. The general manager of the St. Louis Football Cardinals called me the day of my surgery and said, "We are failing you on your physical, and you're now released."

I was in Eugene, Oregon, because I wanted to go to the best Achilles surgeon in the country, and he happened to be there. He'd performed surgery on Mary Decker Slaney and Carl Lewis. After that dismissive call, I couldn't do much. I remember lying in my condo for about a week with the blinds closed, feeling sorry for myself.

Once that week had passed, I told myself, "OK, your life's been nothing but a freaking bed of roses. This is the plan. Something better is going to come because this happened. And I can't see it, I don't know what it is, but . . ." Then I asked the big question, "What am I going to do?"

The answer came right back at me. "You know what? I'm going to talk to that guy John Qualley and see what he thinks."

I talked to John and finally said, "I think I could sell your product."

"I know you could," John said. "You'd be amazing."

I'd already gotten my Series 7 exam in 1985, so I moved my broker's license over. Early on in my new career, I didn't manage much money. I mostly just sold insurance products, but I kept training. For the next two years, while rehabbing, I sold insurance products full time for Northwestern Mutual.

For about six months or maybe even a year, I thought I wasn't going to play again because my situation had not improved. By October of 1989, when I finally realized my Achilles had healed, I was down to 255 pounds, was full time in the business, and really had given up on football. Then I realized, "Wow, I'm healthy. Let's give this a shot again." At the time, I was twenty-seven, about to turn twenty-eight years old, which meant I'd be in the prime of my career. I wanted a comeback.

In April of 1990, after training on my own for the previous six months, I got ahold of the Houston Oilers. They said, "We'd love to have you play for us." They gave me a tryout, and I ended up playing another five seasons while still running my business. In my last two seasons, I was one of the top twenty agents of Northwestern's eight thousand, despite the fact that half the season I was playing football and starting every year.

When One Door Closes

When 1995 rolled around, I decided to retire from football. My last year, I played in Cleveland for a guy named Bill Belichick. Nick Saban was the defensive coordinator, and my line coach was Iowa coach Kirk Ferentz.

Currently a wealth coach for Northwestern Mutual Wealth Management Company, I market under the name Dawson Financial Services, and I'm a financial planner and wealth coach. I've been doing this insurance work since 1995. I've got six full-time employees. I manage a bunch of money, sell a bunch of insurance products, and do fee-based financial planning.

I'm a very delusional optimist and always, always, *always* think things are going to work out. I'm very tenacious and very intense. I think God gave me a good heart, and I'm trying my hardest to use my heart more than anything else. Back in the eighth grade, I realized if I needed to stay up until three in the morning, I'd stay up until three in the morning. I'm just never going to quit.

God gave me a pretty decent mind, so I'm really good at this work stuff. I'm also really good at reading people and effectively communicating. To summarize, I've had two jobs in my life: pro football and insurance. For the first fifteen years or so, I sold insurance. For the last sixteen years or maybe a little longer, I mainly did a conference on financial planning. Most of my company's revenue now comes from managing money.

Northwestern's products are very good—amazing, really—and the tax efficiency is excellent. In an industry in which only 16 percent of people make it for more than five years, I'm still here. So I'm extremely enthusiastic. Sales is the transfer of enthusiasm, so I help people understand how effective and how great our policies are. Everybody's underinsured as relates to life insurance, and nobody saves enough money or has enough tax-efficient ways of growing capital.

Working in the finance business is not like playing football. I can't get in the door unless you let me in. I'm comfortable calling on and speaking to anyone. I like to believe I can connect well with people,

I'm honest, and I'm representing products I believe in. I believe I can transfer my enthusiasm to those with whom I work, and so I do.

The Providence Boardroom

Remember, I wanted to play pro football, and I did not think I was actually finished with that, so I was looking for a career that would give me complete flexibility. I had been making a couple hundred thousand dollars a year. I now had the choice of either getting a job as an engineer for $40,000 or $50,000 a year or finding a job that could bring in $200,000 a year, which I did my second year.

Definitely, I wanted flexibility; I wanted to run my own business; I wanted something I believed in. All those things gave me the passion. And it's been an easy career for me, even though it's a very difficult career for most who attempt it. I like financial planning; I like helping people make those decisions; and I like doing it for myself. All those things added to it—the flexibility, the running my own business, and the great products all appealed to me. However, the name of my boardroom is the Providence Boardroom.

I don't believe in coincidence. I believe in providence. God put in my heart, "This would be a great thing for you to do." I brought in $200,000 in my second year in 1989, and my third year, I made probably $240,000, and the last six months of the year, I played pro football and earned $300,000. I feel blessed to be invited to do speaking engagements, and the FCA organization is one of my favorites. I enjoy seeing young athletes' eyes glazed with optimism for their futures, and I try to bolster their dreams with my own story.

In my first year at UT, some people took me out to get me drunk—sort of an old tradition. I told myself, "I've never been drunk, and I'm not going to drink now." I just poured the beer down my chest, as if I had accidentally spilled it while chugging. Actually, I was pouring the whole thing down there.

One guy looked ready to fight me. "You're not drinking," he accused me.

"Sure I am."

"Then let's do another one!"

"OK."

I poured that beer down my shirt again, and he started getting irate.

Peer pressure can be pretty powerful. Yet we're all trying to do our best, and when it comes down to the bottom line, whom do you want to please? As long as I'm doing my best, I can't help it if I don't please you or I don't please somebody else. All I really want to do is please God.

Delusional Optimism: The Downside

I trained hard and worked hard, and work was like riding a bike. I started as a rookie, and I was really good. But then I had a real bad investment in the late 1990s, and I lost $7 million. That's not a typo: $7 million. I had invested in a lumber mill, and I kept putting money in it, expanding it. Just to make it clear, my delusional optimism is a strength. I know I can accomplish things, and I know I can get everything done. Still, it is also a weakness. I should have shut the freaking thing down after I lost a million dollars. But I kept thinking, *It's going to work out. Nobody's going to steal from me. We're going to be fine.* Once again, I was already in very good financial shape. You have to make a lot to pay back a bunch of money, but it worked out. And compared to somebody's health issues or anything else that's actually important in life . . . Ultimately, it was just money.

The first game I played in the National Football League in 1984 as a rookie was against a guy named Lawrence Taylor, the best defensive player. The first scene in the movie *The Blind Side* was about the left tackle blocking on him. I remember thinking to myself, *This is going to be the most fun I've ever had.* What a challenge! I got to block on Lawrence

Taylor in my first start in college, when I was a freshman at UT and he was a senior at North Carolina. At the end of the day, I told myself, "Hey, I'm gonna pray like it's all up to God and work like it's all up to me."

I think God made me this way and that, with my parents' nurturing, I had a much better chance. A study done in the 1950s by someone in the insurance business found that the number-one indicator of success is not intelligence, and it is not hard work. It's grit. It's never giving up. You're going to get knocked down in any business. Will you get back up? How many times? I think there's only one way to actually have humility, and that is through having reverence, believing in a higher being, and believing in a bigger picture than just yourself.

Role Models

My main role model growing up was my dad, who died of Alzheimer's six years ago. He was a most humble, mild-mannered, and successful patrolling geologist. Everybody I ever met in Houston, Texas, who found out I was Ross Dawson's son—that's what would excite them, not that I was all-American at UT or played four years for the Oilers—said, "He was the nicest, best guy I've ever met."

He coached my Little League teams, and we won two championships in the Spring Branch Independent School District. He was always available, always at our games. We bought a lake house; we had a farm; and Dad put his family, my brother and me, first. We had a really good, very affirming childhood.

I had some great coaches I played for and played under. That goes without saying. However, I had a choir director at my church when I was growing up who was the most hardcore, aggressive, intense perfectionist—a guy who expected so much out of us. Although I wasn't a great singer, the intensity and the passion he had, along with these super high expectations, allowed me to learn so much from him.

Because of the way he approached his life and his profession, he was a major role model for me, someone I really looked up to.

If I could offer only one piece of advice to a younger or less experienced person, it would be this: do not listen to anyone who says you can't do something.

Hal Garwood

Award-Winning Retired Teacher and Coach

"What winning is all about."

When you think about PE class, what do you think about? Jumping jacks and running laps? If so, then you never knew Hal Garwood, my inspiration and the inspiration for many lucky kids over the years. There are many layers to Hal, some of them less obvious than others. He's a proud veteran, a loving husband, a father to his two daughters, and a mentor to the many he trained in numerous innovative, even life-changing ways as a physical education teacher for nearly forty years.

Hal went to school to study business, but after two years at Iowa State, he knew he wanted to be a teacher. He's now retired after more than thirty-eight years of teaching physical education in Cedar Rapids, but he'll never stop motivating kids. It's in his blood.

"As a young person, I was in every sport there was," he told me. "I had plenty to do in high school, interacted with a lot of teachers, and built my confidence up. Some of my coaches had techniques I didn't agree with, and I wanted to improve on them. I always concentrated heavily on fitness. I created obstacle courses, and my kids participated for the Presidential Physical Fitness Award. All the events in gymnastics were taught . . . a city-wide basketball shooting contest . . . a national punt pass and kick competition . . . westside relays with three-legged races, potato-sack relays, and wheelbarrow races." These are activities that sparked interest among both boys and girls.

Hal grew up in a small town where the seasons dictated the activity. In the summer, it was baseball. In the fall, it was football. He always put the focus on sportsmanship.

"I saw it improve as I was teaching," he says. "I saw kids who didn't enjoy the sport unless they were winning."

So the gold medal winner isn't the only person who wins?

"Of course not," Hal says. "You've got hundreds of thousands of people who improved their lives by participating. That's the kind of life I've always led: making new friends, learning rules of the game—that's what winning is all about."

Hal taught me and the rest of the many young people he impacted the basics of sportsmanship. It comes down to respect, he says. "If you knock somebody down, you help them up. After the game, congratulate them. Let them know, 'Good game or match.' And if you didn't win, say something positive: 'I'll get you next time.'"

Nothing about Hal surprises me, but I learned even more about him while writing this book. After two years at Iowa State, he got a three-month job on a Norwegian freighter. Hal worked in the engine room, painting and cleaning. He was able to spend time all over Europe, and he hitchhiked wherever curiosity led him. Hal managed a visit to the World's Fair in Atlantic City before he made his way back to Iowa. You can imagine how this must have impressed a young man from a small town in the farmlands of Iowa.

"I left motivated. I wanted to be the best I can be," he says.

He returned to Urbandale, working for the city as a street sweeper and road grader. He did a little bit of everything. He also worked nights at the Colonial Bakery in Des Moines to make extra money—exactly $2,500, enough to buy a 1965 Ford Galaxy convertible. He finished up his last two years of college at Drake University. Because there were no high school openings, he took a job teaching elementary school in Cedar Rapids.

But then real life came knocking at his door. He received his draft notice in the summer of 1968. By August of the same year, he was at Fort Polk in Louisiana. He came home for Christmas and learned that in January he'd be serving in Vietnam.

"I was a private and advanced to a specialist degree pretty fast," he says, "after a month of infantry in the front lines of battle." Hal later spent an even greater amount of time in charge of the security of the outpost, flying on helicopter missions almost every day.

"There were sniper attacks, and many of our people were killed," he recalls. "VC snuck through barbed wire carrying dynamite. I never slept well again."

He was involved in a helicopter crash when, about halfway back to his company, the engine blew. "We lost our power and went straight down into a rice paddy," Hal says. "All I had was a pistol, and we found our way to another base, where we took another copter to get us out of there." Needless to say, this was a difficult experience for Hal and so many of our other serviceman.

"They asked if I could type. I said I was the best typist in my high school class," he said. "You bet I could type! So, I was company clerk for next six or seven months before I was honorably discharged."

When we met, he was teaching at Van Buren Elementary School in Cedar Rapids, Iowa. Imagine how those experiences had helped shape this young man, who returned to Iowa determined to teach young people to love fitness and develop an interest in sports. That's the guy I encountered when I was just a kid.

Back then, Hal knew students needed more than just PE classes to develop their skills, so he added intramural programs. Ice skating, jump roping, stilt walking, juggling—they were all part of the program. So was tinikling. This traditional Philippine folk dance uses two bamboo poles. Two dancers beat, tap, and slide the bamboo poles on the ground and against each other in coordination with other dancers, who step over and between the poles. Pretty cool compared to regular old PE, isn't it?

Hal developed a team of kids who would go around and perform at high school athletic events, in the recreational parks, and at any venue curious about tinikling. They were a highlight at the nursing homes. This unusual sport attracted attention all over the state, including at universities such as the University of Northern Iowa and several high schools. At one point, he had seventy-two kids performing with thirty poles.

"The kids got so good at tinikling, they added jump roping and twirling hula hoops while keeping the beat between the poles," he says.

Confession: my two sisters and I were members of his tinikler team. Hal says we were pretty good.

He also had thirty to forty kids on his ball-spinning team every year while tinikling.

"I had second- and third-grade kids who could spin balls," he says. "I taught my daughters how to do it. One did it for ten minutes without stopping."

Hal believes you can master just about anything, including ball spinning, if you practice the skill five minutes a day.

"Give it your best. Take pride in whatever effort you give."

Jim Patterson, another PE teacher and lifetime friend of Hal, started the jump-rope team. Prior to that, Hal had worked with a team of mostly girls that came from Marshalltown. In 1991, the team invited Hal to take their jump-roping skills and talents all the way to Australia. He was able to bring his two daughters, who practiced with his team, and spent three weeks in Australia with the Marshalltown Skippers.

Hal knew how to motivate and encourage thousands of kids just to participate, to open their eyes to so many sports and activities. He has long been a member of the Cedar Rapids Ice Skating Hall of Fame and was a member of the Iowa Skippers Jump Rope Team until his retirement.

Students loved him, and he attended more graduations and weddings that he can count. "I've been to hundreds of high school graduations," he told me. "My wife and I still go to several different ball games to support my former students and now even their own kids. I was blessed to have a lot of great kids, and they know I haven't forgotten them. I don't lose track of them."

As you can see, this guy is exploding with Magic Dust qualities. One of his major ones is the ability to bring out the best in others, to help them recognize and achieve their full potential. He has been a loving husband to Carolyn, his wife of nearly fifty years. He demonstrated incredible patience in working with elementary-aged children. His guidance as a male role model was invaluable to thousands of young men, and his passion for teaching is boundless.

His advice to others is simple. "Be the best you can be, find that heartfelt passion to do what you enjoy, and have fun at it."

Hal and I have talked many times about my concept of Magic Dust. He believes some people are born with their own special qualities and— very importantly—that anyone can develop them, no matter what your circumstances may be.

"I was quiet and shy as a boy," he says. "Through hard work and coaching, I found what brought out the best in me, and I feel privileged to have been able to influence others in my lifetime."

Thanks, Coach.

Beau Williford

Ragin' Cajun Boxing Club

"Boxing was his vehicle to impact people's lives."

As I finished this book, my friend Beau Williford lay dying. That was tough. He started boxing at only six years old and was a well-known boxing manager in Lafayette, Louisiana. We met when his boxing club burned down. He was teaching kids out of the carport at his house, and I asked what I could do to help. I was glad to help sponsor the Ragin' Cajun Boxing Club for several years. Beau took kids who were at risk, kept them out of fights at school, and taught them boxing as a sport. Instead of getting expelled for fighting on school grounds, these kids had the opportunity to get a medal or trophy in a match. This wasn't just a local boxing club. Beau brought national Golden Gloves to Lafayette, Louisiana. Beau had national presence. He was a tough guy who always did what he said he was going to do.

Christian, one of Beau's five sons, used to do yardwork for me when he was young. Upon Beau's passing, Christian told me, "One of my dad's last wishes was that you get this book published and that he's in it."

"You don't have to worry about that," I told Christian. "He's in the book. He meant too much to too many people not to include." I know Beau's story will inspire you.

Christian likes to say that his dad never met a stranger. He is so right, and my friendship with Beau is just one example of that. Raised in North Carolina, Beau relocated to Lafayette, Louisiana, with a friend to work the oil fields in 1979. It's good that he did. After arriving, he and a friend attended the twenty-first birthday party of a young woman named Teri. Although he didn't meet her that day, she would later become Beau's wife. A few days later, when one of Teri's friends from high school and college came to visit her, the group went to eat gumbo. Teri had always found big men attractive, and she couldn't help noticing Beau as he walked past her to put something in the garbage.

"Oh, he's big," her friend said.

"And he's cute too," Teri replied.

That's how they met.

"Five kids and forty years later," she told me, shortly after Beau's passing. "It's been quite the ride."

That's right. They had five sons: twins Mabon and Wesley, followed by Christian, Alexander, and Samuel.

"He loved children," Teri said. "That's why I fell in love with him."

Beau did care about kids, and he believed boxing could offer them a path they might not otherwise find. Christian said it best: "Boxing was his vehicle for being able to impact people's lives."

Beau understood that firsthand. In his youth, he had a distinguished amateur career as an aspiring boxer. That led him to New York and a brief professional career. In the days of Muhammad Ali, Joe Frazier, and George Foreman, Beau had a circle of boxing friends and a Rolodex of contacts nationwide in the boxing world. As a family man living in Lafayette, Beau saw the sport as an opportunity to help him give back to the community. Equally important was that he knew the benefits boxing could provide to many at-risk kids. Anybody was welcome at the Ragin' Cajun Boxing Club, but the students who stayed knew it was a place where they could feel special.

Many people don't know that Beau and I became close friends because of a fire, although we probably would have connected sooner or later. I happened to notice in the Lafayette newspaper that the facility Beau had been using had burned down and the boxers were temporarily practicing in the carport of Beau and Teri's driveway. I immediately reached out to see how I could help Beau and his team. Two other boxing enthusiasts, attorneys Glenn Armentor and Tony Fazzio, both former boxers themselves, supported our efforts to find a new facility: a large gym with a workout area and space for a full-size ring.

The club, which closed four months after Beau's death in 2019, sent a team to compete in Ireland; hosted the Louisiana State Silver Gloves and Louisiana Governor's Games annually; helped arrange a visit from Muhammad Ali's trainer, Angelo Dundee; and brought the Louisiana State Golden Gloves back to Acadiana following a twenty-year absence.

Beau was at the gym daily and was always looking to set up fights for his boxers. He was so well regarded by his peers that he was able to convince the regional Golden Gloves organization to let Lafayette become a host city. Coordinating the event was a huge responsibility for Beau. A fire might have brought us together, but once we met, I wasn't going away. Whether it was buying tables at a Golden Gloves event or donating a fifteen-passenger van to the club, I remained a friend and supporter in numerous capacities.

Common Ground

Christian said of his dad, "If he got along with somebody, they quickly became close friends."

That's what happened with Beau and me. I'd always been interested in boxing. When I was thirteen, my dad wanted me to learn how to defend myself, so he sent me to the YMCA to work with John and Drew, the sons of his friend Maury Hachey. Both were skillful and eager to teach what they knew from their own years in the ring. They trained me well, and I felt that I was getting more experience at practice two or three days per week than I did in the three quick rounds in actual boxing bouts. I found boxing was a tough story to sell on the occasions I showed up at school with a fat lip or a shiner, even though they were just training bruises.

Earning trophies and testing your new skills are huge confidence boosters, both in and out of the ring. I believe Beau and I agreed on this. I finally stopped boxing and wrestling, and the rest of my high school sports time was spent playing football, baseball, and basketball. However, I believed—and still do—that boxing is a great way to gain confidence because it teaches you how to protect yourself and also helps you with other sports. Hand and foot speed, reflexes, hand-eye coordination, and learning to be observant of the opponent's tendencies and look for weakness are just a few of the required skills.

When I was in my late twenties, some of us in our church group volunteered at Westley Rankin Community Center in South Oak Cliff, a rough area in Dallas. We decided to hold a boxing tournament, built an official-size ring, found a referee, and recruited a doctor for the day. A twenty-year-old two-time Golden Gloves champion from Dallas decided he wanted to see what I was made of, so even I spent some unplanned time sparring in the ring, proving to myself that once you learn the sport, you never really lose it.

Once you've boxed, you understand the boxer's mentality. Like Beau, I understood that if you get in the ring, you're going to get hit. Knowing that, Beau and I would watch kids in the ring with the perspective of a boxer, not a worried parent. Once that headgear and gloves are on and you are in that ring, ready to rumble, it is just mano a mano. Yes, it is a sport, not a brawl or a slugfest.

Beau enjoyed teaching the art of the punches and jabs, looking for the opening for the hook, and coming forward for an open uppercut. Beau was a technical coach and drew praise from other coaches nationwide as he brought boxers to regional and national Golden Gloves, including his own son Christian, a natural who showed his skills in the ring with true finesse. Beau even helped boxers turn professional—that is, get paid.

Yet Beau made sure the boxers were learning to box for the sport and told each one that no fighting at school would be tolerated. If you got in trouble, then you would not fight in a tournament. Schoolwork and grades were also important to Beau, and he always had good things to say about his student athletes.

"These kids get better grades since they want to box," he told me. "And grades come first."

Beau had a group of good people helping him, but he had the best support at home with Teri, who worked a full-time banking job and was the breadwinner for the family. Teri Williford says she wishes she'd had a guestbook in their home because it's almost impossible to remember all the houseguests Beau invited to stay with them over the years.

"I can't even count the number of people who lived with us or visited from out of town," she said. "Somebody would move out, and a friend of ours would say, 'The vacancy light is on. I wonder how long it's going to be before somebody moves in.'"

Beau had well-known boxing celebrities like Oscar De La Hoya and Roy Jones Jr. stop in Lafayette to visit. He waited until the last minute to tell Teri they had a new guest arriving.

"He knew I wasn't going to be that happy," she said. "Not because I didn't care, because I did, but because I had kids to take care of and a full-time job."

One day, he told Teri, "This boxer is coming from Ireland."

"When?" Teri asked, not thrilled.

"Tomorrow."

"Thanks a lot. What's his name?"

"Her name," he told Teri. "A woman boxer."

Deirdre Gogarty-Morrison was the boxer, and she and Teri remain dear friends today. Deirdre had dreamed of becoming a boxer, but in Ireland, women weren't allowed to box, although that has changed dramatically in the last twenty years. She wrote letters appealing to boxers all over the United States because she felt her best chance of a career was here. Someone told her about Beau and said, "He knows everything there is to know about boxing."

Nine months passed, and one day, Beau called her out of the blue. He said he didn't know anything about women's boxing and didn't want to learn, but he invited her to come train with him.

"I came over, and he ended up being the best manager and trainer, taking me all the way to a world title," Dierdre said. "Beau was a big, tough, strong guy who told you straight up exactly what he thought."

He wasn't an easy trainer, but he was a great one.

"He said he'd train me like a man because that was the only way he knew. He'd send me out running at five in the morning, following in the suburban, honking and making me go faster until he was convinced I'd do it on my own." Although she was intimidated at first, Dierdre soon learned that Beau was her greatest ally. "He became a big protector of mine and wouldn't let anybody take advantage of me. To protect one of his own fighters, he would go to blows if he had to."

Beau, Dierdre told me, was also a great cut man; he had a special knack for stopping a cut from bleeding.

He got her a fight in Kansas City and drove fourteen hours each way even though they barely knew each other. According to Dierdre, they would "fight anybody anywhere," and winning the world title was their greatest victory.

"It was my third and final attempt at trying to win," she said. "Beau had me running five miles a day for six weeks straight."

Today, twenty years later, that fight is still considered the standard of women's boxing.

When Dierdre remembers Beau's Magic Dust qualities, she thinks of words like *strong* and *firm*. "One of the greatest gifts he had," she said, "was the ability to see potential in you no matter who you were."

When I started this book, Beau was notified he would be getting a call for an interview to review his story for inclusion. During the end of our interviews, Beau had to reschedule a couple of times, and we learned that his cancer had taken a turn for the worse. Beau passed away while I was writing the book, but thanks to Teri, Christian, and Diedre, his chapter is here. I hope he motivates you as he did all the others around him.

Just two years before writing this book, I was sitting in a diner in Lafayette, discussing the list of boxing items Beau needed to order for the gym. While we sat there, a couple of loud-speaking younger gentlemen came inside. Beau couldn't take it any longer and said, "Hey, guys, you mind piping it down? We're having a conversation over here."

They started whispering to each other, and Beau said. "Hey, those guys are just a couple of punks. We could easily kick their asses."

The man was not afraid to speak his mind.

Beau had many Magic Dust qualities. He was sincere. He really cared about his boxers. He had compassion, and he was authentic. Beau was truly a steward of the sport of boxing, a community role model, a loving father, and a true friend, and he had so much to live for. When Beau took the last official eight count, his passing was a true loss to boxing.

After his death, many expressed what he had meant to them. One young man said Beau saved him from taking his own life. I know that the world of boxing and the world in general are better places because of Beau Williford. Our hearts and sympathy go out to Teri Williford and her boys, with special thanks to Christian.

Erin Young Garrett

Collegiate Basketball Player, Real
Estate Professional, and Mom

"I think it goes back to your life purpose."

Not many folks would just walk onto the University of Southern
California campus looking to try out for the basketball team, let alone
a slender young woman from the comfortable Dallas neighborhood
of Highland Park. Yet that is exactly what Erin Young did after not
getting recruited to play college basketball. She figured she would go
big and show the USC Trojans what everybody else was missing out
on. Erin made the team and enjoyed a solid four-year collegiate career.

She later returned home to Dallas and met a widower with four
children. They now have two children of their own, to make a family
of six siblings. Her husband, Judd Garrett, played and coached for the
Dallas Cowboys organization. Erin has never been one to back down
from a challenge, personally or professionally, and she is a motivator
on so many levels.

Erin's Story

By Erin Young Garrett

I think everyone has their own Magic Dust, something unique about them. It's the essence of each individual, the way each of us does things, that quality you have to find within yourself. When you are in tune with that, you really get results.

I was born and raised in Dallas but wanted to do something really different after that. I applied to various colleges far from home and ended up at the University of Southern California. Heading the opposite direction from my safety zone to study public policy at USC was scary for me, and I didn't know what to expect. I went on a whim, not knowing what I was getting into.

I was playing basketball for USC, and after my freshman year, they gave me a scholarship. After those four years, I was the only one of the class I came in with who stuck with playing on the team. I was a captain my senior year. That's part of the Magic Dust Mark talks about. You do what you have to do, even if—and especially if—you don't know how it's going to turn out.

I come from a very strong, very close family, and being so far from their support when I moved to California was really different for me. I also came from a much more traditional background than most of my Californian classmates. When my mom and my older brother moved me in my freshman year, a guy six feet in front of me didn't hold the door open for me, and I was shocked.

"He actually stood there and looked around at me," I told my brother. "He saw that I had a box in my hand, and he didn't even hold the door for me. I can't believe it."

Looking back, that guy was probably as stressed as I was, but it was the first time in my life something like that had happened. That's how protected I was.

After college, I thought I wanted to go into sports marketing, but the team I was working for went on strike, so I moved back to Dallas and got into real estate sales. I sold luxury condominium spaces at the W Dallas and W Austin Hotel and Residences. Then I headed for New York University and earned my master's degree in urban planning. When my father was diagnosed with terminal cancer, I came home. Both my parents worked in residential and commercial real estate, so I went into those. I met Mark Harris through a project, and we just stayed in touch, probably because we share many of the same values.

Love and Other Challenges

I come from a sports family. My brother played major league baseball. When I met Judd Garrett, I knew he was special. Both he and his brother, Jason Garrett, had moved all over because their dad was a coach in the NFL. Jason, a coach and former player, is the offensive coordinator for the New York Giants. Before that, he served as the head coach of the Dallas Cowboys. A college football quarterback at Princeton University, Jason also played for the Cowboys, New York Giants, Tampa Bay Buccaneers, and Miami Dolphins.

Judd had been a running back in the NFL for the Dallas Cowboys. He also was a member of the Las Vegas Posse in the Canadian Football League and the London Monarchs in the World League of American Football.

Judd was married with four kids, aged four to fourteen years old, when his wife Kathy passed away suddenly. Just like that, he had to rearrange his life and decided to take a step back in his career to take care of them. Nine years later, Judd and I met through Jason and his wife, Brill. I was thirty-four and pretty happy with who I was. Sure, I wanted kids, but if it wasn't with the right person, I wasn't going to do it.

Judd had not dated between the time of his wife's passing and meeting me. He was focused on work and the kids. At the time, I was taking care of my dad and wasn't sure I was up to the challenge of dating anyone, let alone anyone fourteen years older with four kids. I just wasn't sure I could take on that responsibility. Not ideal circumstances, right?

After spending time with Judd, however, I felt something similar to what I felt when I took the chance to attend USC. I felt on the right path. You have to have confidence and be grounded in that confidence. That's the Magic Dust—knowing who you are, even if you don't know where you're going to end up.

Judd and I dated for a year and a half. Once we got married, he was able to move forward with his coaching career. Now, we have not only those four kids but two more, for a total of three boys and three girls.

When you can figure out, at the core, who you are, you can do the right thing. A lot of my core beliefs are based on my Christian faith. You do the right thing. You always take the high road. You watch people cheat the system, and you feel cheated at the time. But we all know life is a marathon, and it's the legacy you're leaving behind that counts. As I raise a one- and a two-year old, I know that it doesn't matter what I say to them. It's what they watch me do that's going to affect them the most and mold them into the man and woman they will be come.

No major decision in life is going to be easy. When I met Judd, I had lots of reservations. I also had a strong sense of faith, and I knew with my heart I was with the right person at the right time. When I got out of my comfort zone and attended USC, I found a level of confidence and self-esteem I couldn't have gotten anywhere else. My relationship with Judd felt similar. Although I was overwhelmed at times, I also believed I was on the right path. When you marry, whatever the circumstances, you have to have faith in who your partner is as a person. There's no way you can know for sure. Yes, I was very scared, but I knew he was the one. I was hesitant because this was a full plate to take on.

Shared Passion

Judd is a wonderful writer, and I believe athletes and writers have a lot in common. When you step on the court or get in that mode, everything else goes away, and you just do what you do. You aren't thinking about anything else. You have to figure out how to score, and that's where creativity under pressure comes in. Of course, you need the skills you've practiced, but you also have to have the passion and focus.

You have to have Magic Dust.

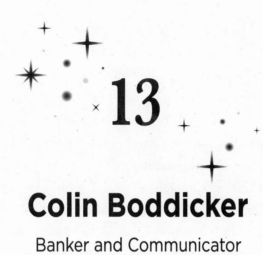

Colin Boddicker

Banker and Communicator

"Communication and follow-through."

I met Colin on a tour of the Dallas Cowboys' practice facilities given by the husband of a good friend. The tour guide was Judd Garrett, and it was after 5:00 pm. Judd is the brother of Jason Garrett, who at the time of our tour was head coach. As I arrived at the Cowboy headquarters, called "the Star," I noticed a tall tree standing in the middle of the lobby. And as I got closer, I realized the six-feet-nine tree happened to be Colin Boddicker, who was also there to take the tour. Once he said his last name, bells went off. That name is famous in Iowa, where both Colin and I were raised. Colin lit up when I asked if he was kin to Mike, the MLB pitcher who grew up in Norway, Iowa, or to Dan, the highly regarded defensive end for the Iowa Hawkeyes back in the mid-1980s, when they ranked as high as number one in the nation.

"Yes, I am," said Colin, and I knew we would be instant friends. Colin was a respectable basketball player himself while at Texas Christian

University. Erin Garrett, whom you met in the previous chapter, and Colin both served as volunteer coaches for a private school in Dallas. Colin knew Chris, Erin's brother, who went onto play major league baseball. Colin was in wealth management financial planning and was there for the tour along with Erin and her husband, Judd. As most of my friends know, I'm a huge Cowboys fan. Colin likes the Cowboys, but he's a big sports fan in general.

Colin develops comprehensive wealth management and private banking solutions for high-net-worth families and business owners. In his spare time, he's a color commentator on radio and TV for Texas Christian University basketball games. His love for basketball and sports are true passions that give him confidence, and his confidence makes him a great motivator.

Colin's Story

By Colin Boddicker

When I think about Magic Dust, I see it as how you harness your talents to set yourself up for success. It's no secret that I'm a big sports fan. I love the drive and desire you have to possess to make it as a professional.

I played basketball in college at Texas Christian University from 1999 to 2002. Until 2010, when TCU won the Rose Bowl, not many knew about us. In addition to the Rose Bowl exposure, a lot of alumni became bigger donors. The endowment grew, and the university did a good job of spending the endowment funds wisely, including on facility and stadium upgrades and new buildings all over campus.

When I graduated from college, I probably could have played basketball in some very small lower-level leagues, but I didn't want to do that. The members of my graduating class were the first in the country with a tech-focused business degree. But then the dot-com bubble burst, and people who had ten to fifteen-plus years of coding experience couldn't find jobs. So, in the fall of 2002, I packed up everything I owned, including a stack of resumes and my double degree in finance and e-business, and moved to Laguna Niguel, California, where my brother lived.

No longer focused on e-business, I went down the career path in financial planning I had originally preferred. Once I got to California, I realized I faced a major challenge breaking into that industry. The question I encountered time and again was, "Who do you know?"

The business is all about contacts. Other than my brother and his friends, I didn't know anybody. After about four months of spinning my wheels, I didn't find any career path that appealed to me. I came back to Texas, and in a week and a half, I had a job.

Those four months in California amounted to a humbling experience. I'd been a good student my entire life. I'd excelled athletically enough to play in college, and I wasn't used to not achieving a goal I set my mind to. To get out of school and then get knocked down in the real world was a nice wake-up call. The first thing you do when you get knocked down is get back up. The next thing you do is figure out how you got knocked down so it doesn't happen again.

Communication Matters

When you're talking to clients about their investments, you have to communicate to them about what's going on and why. If the market's taken a tough downturn, you must communicate even more effectively. Communication—rather, the lack of it—is the number-one reason clients change financial advisers. Clients see investments go up and down, so they think advisers don't add any value. They typically change advisers only when that adviser hasn't called the client—and often when another adviser does.

Success in our business is all about communication and follow-through. The ones who get weeded out are the ones who don't communicate and the ones who don't follow through. Folks who do that have an infinite amount of success. It's all about being engaged.

There comes a time in an adviser's career when they can be selective about who they take on. But if you are building your career and want to get the business, you've got to pick up the phone. My first job was in strategic wealth management, but because I worked for an insurance company, the financial planning was insurance driven. Because I didn't want to be labeled a job hopper and didn't want to jump ship right away, I stayed there two years. I wasn't excited about the higher-pressure sales. As soon as I got to that two-year mark, I left, but my experience there gave me an opportunity to learn a very important skill that I think a lot of people today are lacking. I learned how to pick up the phone and call people.

The art of being able to carry a conversation on the phone is being lost among the next generation. They think it's more efficient to shoot texts and emails back and forth, yet when I get an email chain, I have to go back and see what was said. It's so much easier for me to pick up the phone and just ask. My clients like getting a phone call more than a text message. Using the phone is an underrated skill. If you have it, you'll have a leg up on everyone else in any business you're in.

I admire people's work ethic more than anything. To do what you say you're going to do, you have to have a work ethic. Some prefer to call this integrity.

I typically do my workouts early in the morning, but I have to get my work done before I go to the gym. I commit to both the job and the workout, and I know the order in which they will happen.

Regardless of where you are in your career, just learn how to talk to people. Strike up conversations with strangers. You will learn so much more about people by having conversations with them. As I said before, you have to be able to communicate and pick up the phone. Communication isn't just about business. It's about how you deal with your parents, your siblings, and your significant other. And it's all about being able to convey what you're thinking. Even more importantly, it's about what the person on the other end of the phone is thinking.

14

Debbra Raymer

Senior Executive Assistant

"Everybody's Magic Dust is different . . ."

My sister Debbra Raymer, along with her husband, Greg, are motivators in what I call the sanctity of society. Deb and Greg—and those like them—personify the spiritual and emotional glue that holds together marriage, family, and relationships both personal and professional.

Deb's Story

By Debbra Raymer

In our family, I am the eldest child of three siblings. At sixteen and eighteen, our parents were literally teenagers themselves when they married. Though my parents were young, they instilled in me the basics: work hard to move forward in life; understand that life is not fair, so don't expect it to be; to survive, you must work at something.

These basic values have been proven to me over and over again in my lifetime. I am here to say it's been a journey. I share no regrets, and let me tell you why. From listening and watching my younger brother Mark, I have learned—and believe—that we all have the potential for our own Magic Dust. After watching my brother set his goals and achieve them time after time, I started to understand that he just knows his skills and sticks to what he is good at.

After years of conversations and years of performing my own job responsibilities, I now realize my own Magic Dust is different from Mark's—different from anyone else's, actually. I am a loving sister, committed wife, caring stepmom, awesome aunt, loyal senior executive assistant, trustworthy friend, and helpful neighbor. I have enjoyed sprinkling my Magic Dust in all of those roles. We all have choices to make about how we decide to give of ourselves and what we make of ourselves.

I am actually eighteen months older than my brother Mark. Our younger sister, Dawn, is four years younger than me. We came from a modest family, but we still had to work hard. Nobody gave us anything, and we made the most of every opportunity we had.

After starting as an administrative assistant, I worked my way up to senior executive assistant at a large company in Fort Worth. I've enjoyed this company for almost thirty years, and I see no reason to leave. My employer has been good to me, and I believe the company values my experience and abilities. I love the people I work with, and that's the biggest part of why I've stayed this long. As I've said often, you spend too much time at work to be doing something you don't like with people you don't enjoy. You put in too much time and effort to be doing anything other than what you're passionate about.

Although I never intended to be an executive assistant, it's worked out for me. I make a good living, and I enjoy it. I appreciate this environment, which I am fortunate to be a member of, because everyone is respectful and professional.

More than anything, though, I love my family. Family is everything.

My parents divorced after twenty-one years of marriage, which is probably one of the reasons I value the stability of family so much. My husband and I are happy, and after twenty-four years of marriage I can honestly say I would gladly marry him again. We share many common interests; we enjoy time spent outside and are both big fans of sports, including our beloved Dallas Cowboys and Dallas Mavericks. We enjoy all our family get-togethers for holidays, birthdays, weddings, graduations. Some of our best memories together with family began at lake house reunions. Greg and I can just relax and not go anywhere on many weekends after the forty to fifty hours we spend between driving and work. We have traveled to Hawaii and New York for fun but have spent more time traveling to visit family in Colorado, Wisconsin, Louisiana, and Iowa.

Mark and I feel the same way about family. He is a wonderful father. He knows his kids so well it's unbelievable. And he loves his nieces and nephews too. He is a good man with a big heart. He wants to do something for everybody and has been extremely generous.

Mark may have been blessed to earn a good living, but in my eyes, his generosity and taking on of responsibilities are greater examples of Magic Dust. Yes, this was what we learned as kids growing up: you take care of your family, and family takes care of you.

Sports are a big thing in our family. All three of us siblings played sports in school. Those bonds are still there, as both Greg and I have nieces and nephews who are active in sports today. I love kids a lot. Mark and our sister, Dawn, have been really great about sharing their kids with me, and I have a stepson, Chad, who owns my heart. I love him to pieces. Before Chad and I got to meet, I had to find his dad first. Here's how that happened.

I went to a dance club one night. I was there with a friend, and another guy, Greg, was also there with a friend. When I saw him standing there, I realized he was good looking, and I knew he had noticed me. Still, Mr. Popularity was kind of ignoring me because several other girls were passing his way, trying to get his attention. On my way to the bathroom, I intended to just pass by him, but the place was crowded, and somebody happened to bump me into his six-feet-four body. I believe it was fate.

"Excuse me," I said. Greg just smiled.

When I came out of the restroom, he was standing nearby with his buddy, having a drink.

I tapped him on the shoulder and said, "Do you ever ask anybody to dance, or do they ask you all the time?"

He smiled. "They always ask me."

"OK," I told him. "Bye."

As I started to walk away, he grabbed my arm and said, "If I asked you to dance, what would you say?"

And I said, "I guess you'd have to ask me."

"Well then, I'm asking. Would you like to dance?"

The rest is history.

Greg and I dated for a couple of years before we got married. Greg knew I loved kids, and he was afraid that once I met his son Chad, I might fall in love with him first, which was probably true. Greg didn't want to rush into anything. He had already told me he wasn't going to expose Chad to anybody he dated because he didn't want to confuse him. When he asked me to meet his son, I knew for sure that we had something real happening between us.

Once I did meet Chad, we hit it off right away, and he told his dad he was going to marry me.

"Well," I asked him, "Where's Dad going to live? Where are we going to live?"

"We'll live in your apartment," Chad said. "And we'll visit Dad at his house."

He was just three years old when I met him. He's twenty-nine as I write this and has a degree in computer engineering.

Because my parents divorced after twenty-one years, I'd always said that if I were ever in a situation like this, I would never force a child to call me "Mom." I wanted to be Chad's friend. As I told him, "You're my boy in my heart, *and* you have a mom. I'm here to be your friend, and I love you." We have a great relationship to this day.

My own mom is my role model. She got married at a very young age, and she was a stay-at-home mom because that's what she and my dad had agreed upon. She was a good mom, and she did the very best she could with what she had. She took responsibility for her kids. Her family was important to her. She made sure we went to church every week, and she was always at our sporting events. All of our friends called her "Mom" or "Jo Mom," and I admired the fact that she would try to make other kids feel at home. Furthermore, she loved us, and she encouraged us in every way.

As my mom always said, life isn't fair. That was one of the things she always reminded us of. Not everything's going to go your way, and you have to work for what you get. You should never think that it's going to be handed to you. When you fall, remember: getting up builds character.

Everybody has Magic Dust. Everybody's Magic Dust is different. Everybody has value. Everybody has their own Dust to share. Make the best with what you have. Work hard. Don't give up. And be honest with yourself. You are good enough just being you.

Finally, remember that everybody you meet plays a part in your life, whether you believe it or not.

15

Greg Raymer

Mr. Reliable

"It's all about responsibility."

Greg's Story

By Greg Raymer

I grew up in a military family with a father who gave thirty years to our country before retiring as a chief master sergeant. My dad was in the air force, and for those thirty years, we moved about every four years on average—not just to new towns but many times to new countries and continents. Your childhood affects who you become and sets the course for your adult life. Growing up as a military brat, I was used to making new friends from base to base. I never felt the long-term friendship bonds that I found when I married my wife. We have stability, family, and more shared values than I can count. The stability is especially important to me.

Although I got the chance to meet all kinds of different people, when I listen to Deb, Dawn, and Mark talk about their childhood friends, I realize I never had that kind of long-term stability. As a kid growing up in the 1960s and 1970s, I didn't have the internet. I didn't have social media. None of us did. I had only pencil and paper. I'd meet people, and we'd be friends for four years, and then one of us would move. "Oh yeah, we'll write," we would tell each other, but that was the end of the connection and the friendship.

However, my father's dedication to the military and to the United States was important to me. I lived in the Philippines and Germany when I was a child, as well as all over the States, including California, Louisiana, and Michigan, where I graduated from high school in 1980. After graduation, I worked odd jobs and went to a skills center to train as a welder. My interest and passion in working with tools and my hands led me to learn about metalworking and welding. Once I got my certification, I heard that the oil fields were booming in Texas.

Welding jobs were everywhere in Texas; that's all my fellow welders talked about. When I graduated in 1981, there were no welding jobs in Michigan. Fortunately, my father was transferred to Fort Worth, so I tagged along. By the time I got there in June of 1982, the welding jobs had dried up. I ended up working at U-Haul, welding hitches. It wasn't for me, so I decided to go into the air force as a welder. I guess you can say I was following in my dad's footsteps. Unlike my dad, though, I put in only four years.

Ironically, the welding job the air force promised me never came through, and I would have had to wait a year before that job opened again. Instead, they let me pick another job. I picked machinist, which was probably a good thing for me. While serving, I learned valuable lessons that are part of my everyday life: loyalty, respect, honor, commitment, and dedication. These are not just words but values to live by.

Being a responsible person was something I learned through the military but even more so through being a father myself. I still wake up early, the way I did in my military days, which served me well in my work life as an employee of twenty-eight years in the oil field service. The company relied on me to be early to work to get my department going. My wife of twenty-four years has also gotten accustomed to my early-to-bed, early-to-rise way of life. We enjoy our daily coffee in the mornings and both have given our loyalty to our employers. We are committed to each other and to our families. People know that when I say I will do something or be somewhere, they can count on me.

Respect is demanded in the military. Rank and file follow orders and keep structure among the many armed forces personnel. In the civilian world, it seems, respect comes with proving yourself. I know I respect people who honor their words and follow through on their plans.

Fulfilling Work

After working as a machinist for a long time, I worked my way up through the ranks and became a shop supervisor in drilling, where we rebuilt mud-lubricated motors on the oil rigs that drilled holes in the ground. Then, in 2016, the oil field went downhill. They had to cut back, so they ended up laying me off before they relocated about a year later.

That was a business decision, one I totally understood. I don't have any hard feelings. I've had to lay people off. It's business. It turned out to be a blessing because I got the opportunity to be a director of facility operations in one of Mark's hospitals. My duties included taking care of maintenance of the building, directing housekeeping, managing the landscape contractor, and keeping up with the manuals per regulations. I've been there four years now, as I write this, and I like the total change of pace.

In addition to the maintenance tasks, I also communicate with the patients and staff. I find this extremely fulfilling. I like talking to the patients and listening to their stories. The majority of them are elderly, so I get to listen to people who have witnessed history—for example, one ninety-four-year-old man who was in World War II.

For me, my role model is my dad. He's eighty-three and a hard worker. From the time he was seventeen years old, he grew up in the military— for thirty years! After that, he went to work at Lockheed Martin, where he put in another thirty years. Five years ago, he retired at seventy-eight years old, so he's worked all his life. He's been such a positive role model for me in terms of sports, getting me active, and just teaching me about responsibility. He taught me the value of hard work and not quitting.

Debbie and I went to the school of hard knocks and worked our way up through the ranks, and we're each successful in our own way. That's part of the Magic Dust: doing it your own way and working hard.

I like to think I have lived a simple life. I enjoy the days we can spend just sitting out on our back patio and the weekends we take our camper out to a peaceful piece of land just to enjoy the open air. I enjoy living in Texas. That's why I raised my family here—and value the family I gained through marriage.

Many people think of Magic Dust as something others have that makes them rich, but I like to think Magic Dust might be as simple as the goals that many people strive to attain but don't always achieve. My years of being a faithful, respectful, committed, loyal, honorable husband, as well as an obedient son and reliable friend, might just be my Magic Dust.

Thank you, Debbie, for being my partner and best friend. She has helped remind me of the simple things we do, such as saving from each paycheck for emergencies and opportunities that might come up. We have security in our future from making choices that allow us to live a comfortable and stable lifestyle.

Work hard. Don't give up. Life happens. There are going to be ups and downs, but you just have to plow your way through it. Find and hold on to your **Magic Dust**.

Part IV

WARRIORS

It is challenging for me to describe those individuals who have endured incredible setbacks yet have some of the best personalities you will ever know. They are people who rise above their circumstances and who, in doing so, make us realize the warrior we all have within.

Abbie Harris

Future ASL Sign Language Interpreter

"Just be your best."

Let's start with the youngest person in this book—someone who was handed a life-threatening challenge on only her third day of existence. Abbie was born a healthy, happy-looking baby on day one. On day two, she was sent home to begin her life. The morning of day three included an emergency visit to the hospital. Abbie barely had a pulse when Dr. Mike Judice arrived and told her father her diagnosis was a meningitis virus. It required a spinal tap of this three-day-old baby.

"She may not make it."

Dr. Mike didn't hesitate. "You will hold her while I take the fluid from her spine. We could paralyze her if I miss the fluid cavity."

Dr. Mike's diagnosis was correct, and he had already been in touch with NICU units in Houston and New Orleans. However, the risk of a CareFlite combined with the growing pressure on her brain from fluid swelling was not going to allow her to travel. This was the beginning of daily discussions between physicians and nurses and her father. "Just be prepared, because she may not make it," the shift would remind him each day and night.

Abbie had regular fevers as high as 105 degrees, and Dr. Mike suggested this might result in long-term cognitive issues that may not be noticeable until she was two or three years old. Once again, Dr. Mike was correct. After he saved her life by catching the meningitis diagnosis and immediately starting meds, he was also the one who started to notice Abbie's delay in processing commands.

I was that father. Abbie is my daughter. Over the next ten days of her life—with those constant notifications of her expected death—nurses transferred her from ice beds to incubators, and there were tubes running all over her tiny four-and-a-half-pound body. That experience truly shaped my life. Nothing had ever scared me as much; the outcome was totally out of my hands. I asked God not to make her suffer, and I prayed for what my family and I have today: the opportunity to share Abbie's life.

You've never known helplessness until a medical professional looks you in the eye and tells you that your newborn daughter might not make it. Things got easier for me in business after Abbie survived because I thought, *Man, I'm never again going to face anything as rough as the thought of losing a child.*

Abbie has always been a high-functioning person, athletic enough to be on regular sports teams. She was eventually able to process information at 75 percent when somebody read aloud to her. As I write this book in 2020, Abbie is twenty-two and has discovered her Magic Dust in the ASL field. She started taking sign language classes in ninth grade, has now pursued her degree as an ASL interpreter, and will enjoy working with young students in school settings. This is in no small part due to Dr. Mike's own Magic Dust—not only his devotion to his profession as a pediatrician but his patience in handling this highly stressful situation when Abbie was so young, lethargic, jaundiced, and close to dying.

In just a moment, I'm going to let Abbie tell you her story from her perspective. First, I'd like to tell you how proud I am of her—and of all my kids. I raised them with an entrepreneurial spirit. When they were younger, they wanted to set up a lemonade stand in front of the gate leading to our home, and I completely supported their efforts. There were ten acres stretching beyond that gate, and maybe most kids living in a house like that didn't want to sell lemonade, but my kids did.

Right off, a woman drove up and said, "Do you know the people who own that house, and do they know you're selling lemonade in their driveway?"

"Yes," Abbie said. "We live here, and our dad said we could sell right here." Of course, I was parked behind the front gate in a golf cart, listening. It was a typical hundred-degree day in Lafayette, Louisiana, and I thought they had a great idea. It wasn't about how much they made; it was about instilling in them the excitement of finding and filling a need.

Next a man pulled up in his truck, but he was just as clueless as the woman had been.

"Do the people who live here know you're sitting in their driveway?" he demanded.

Zoe, my second oldest, said, "Yes, sir. It's our house, sir."

"Well, if you live here, then why are you out here selling lemonade?" the guy said.

My proud father ego couldn't take any more. I jumped from the golf cart and proceeded to open the front gate.

"They are out here because they live here," I told the man. "They need to understand that it's work like this that will help them afford a home like this one when they grow up."

He quickly agreed, and I hope he left a little wiser.

My kids remember nonstop activity from their childhood: Home Depot workshops, grocery shopping, discussing what caught their attention about a product, board games, hide-and-go-seek (our favorite), and numerous outdoor sports activities. "Business days" were when the kids offered services, from cleaning a room to practicing "selling" the family silverware (while explaining why it was better than other silverware).

Ironically, although I never discussed the day to day of my business at home, all my kids are now interested in helping others.

I've already told you what being Abbie's dad has been like for me. Abbie is an inspiration. Now, I'd like to turn it over to Abbie.

Abbie's Story

By Abbie Harris

My dad and Dr. Mike Judice saved my life. I've heard the story from the time I was old enough to understand it. I know I could have died if I had moved so much as a muscle as my dad held me down on that table while the doctor did a spinal tap. That was my beginning. I've heard the story so many times that it feels like a memory.

Everything I've dealt with since was caused by meningitis and my 105-degree fever. I don't have a diagnosis of any disability. Still, I have to work hard with reading and math. Although school has been difficult at times, it's OK. I have learned math and reading are important to many things we do every day in life, but I still struggle with both.

I'm always happy to take on a new challenge. When my dad taught me to drive, I freaked out at first, because he made me learn in his truck, the way he taught all of us kids. When I got my car, it was so much easier, and I love driving so much that I've already put more than ninety thousand miles on my car.

My parents are both such strong individuals, and I'm very close to them. I have four siblings. I was always the quiet child who kept to herself, and that's helped me understand kids, who are my passion. I found that connection with my family in my early teens. Other people treat me differently, but not my family. That's why my bond to them is so close.

I work at a preschool, where I lead the kids in activities. I also work independently at times with one little girl. Some of the first words kids say are "mom" and "dad," and she hasn't said either in her entire life. I hope to teach her those two words in sign language.

I was born and raised in Lafayette, Louisiana. By the time I was eight years old, I knew I was behind. My parents started putting me in extra activities and got an occupational therapist and speech specialist to work with me. I also had extra help in class. Yet I have a job. I drive. I work. My parents showed me how to work for what I want.

I learned to sign as a freshman in high school. It came in handy when I was sixteen and had to have jaw surgery to realign my bite. My mouth was nearly closed for four weeks, and I was fed through a straw. My front teeth were not aligned, and I had screws in my jaw, which was scary. I lost thirty pounds. Since I couldn't talk with that rubber band on my teeth, I learned how to sign. I received a few awards for my ASL progress and felt I had found something I really liked. I was pretty good at it. Most of all, I was grateful I could communicate.

Magic Dust: that's the love you show and that you give. That's what my dad does. Whenever I have a bad day, I call him. I look at what people do in their lives that makes them happy. I like to look at their hearts, their joy, and the life that they've grown.

What would you be doing if you weren't working in the field you are?

All my dogs have been rescued. If I weren't working with kids, I'd be working at a dog rescue.

I look up to my sisters, Morgan and Zoe, and to my mom and dad, of course. They're all very smart and protective of me. I am a big sister to my brother Tanner and younger sister Sophie. They have always treated me with love, and all my siblings accept me for who I am. I love how they have always been there for me and how they follow their dreams. The people I admire have always reached their goals, and that's what I want to do.

Achieve your dreams and your goals in life. Don't give up, no matter what anyone else says. If you don't reach your goals right away, that's fine. Just be your very best.

Tom Udstuen

Logistics Manager

"Going the extra mile."

Meet Tom, my little brother (from the Big Brothers Big Sisters program). As you'll soon see, his Magic Dust is that regardless of what life throws at him, he's a survivor. Despite losing his father at age six and dealing with his own health challenges at a young age, Tom is well liked by everybody who knows him, and he has given me the inspiration and motivation to be a successful businessman. His employers hugely praise Tom for always being a positive, happy person. I'll always be grateful that when I met my "Little" more than thirty years ago, it was this guy.

Tom's Story

By Tom Udstuen

I grew up in the Lakewood and Forest Hills area of Downtown Dallas. Those early years in that nice neighborhood with my mother, father, two sisters, and brother were great. My father, Thomas, was an architect, and my mother, Sally, was a stay-at-home mom. When she was only twelve years old, she lost her own parents and was adopted by her aunt and uncle in Beaumont, Texas. She graduated from the University of Texas at Austin with a degree in fashion design and met my dad, who designed what would become our home in Forest Hills.

In the late 1970s, Dad was diagnosed with lung cancer. He passed away in 1980 at the young age of forty-four. Mom was only forty-one at the time. My older sister was fifteen, my brother was thirteen, and my younger sister was eight. I was six.

In 1985, when I was eleven, we moved to Richardson, another suburb of Dallas, where the public school system was highly regarded at the time. I finished elementary school, junior high, and high school there. About that time, my mom thought I needed a role model, which I'm sure I did. My biological brother, Steve, was eighteen and had already moved out of the house to pursue his new adult life. She enrolled me in the Big Brothers Big Sisters program, and it changed my life.

Around the same time, Mark Harris had moved down here from Iowa and was working for a computer company, MicroSolutions. He wanted to do some good for the community, so he decided to volunteer as a Big Brother in the same program in which my mom had just enrolled me. That's how we got matched up. He's been my "Big" from BBBS for thirty-something years now. We tell that story at the Big Brothers Big Sisters Golf Tournament he sponsors each year, and it always gets a few looks of amazement.

From ages eleven to nineteen, my life was good, and much of that was because Mark was always around. We would get together for an activity usually once a month, maybe twice a month, off and on throughout the year, including the Big Brothers Big Sisters bowling events. The BBBS program requires you to stay in it for only eighteen months. Mark always reminds me of that, and he always jokes to people, "Yeah, Tom and I met thirty-something years ago. I was only contracted for eighteen months, and I still can't get rid of him."

In 1986, my mother was diagnosed with MS, and we saw her grow weaker by the year. I remember my mom and Mark sitting in the stands at my baseball games in the middle of summer heat and at my basketball games. She started with a cane, then went to a walker, and next to a wheelchair to get around.

I graduated from high school and worked at my best friend's father's law firm during the summer and into the fall and winter. November of 1993, the year I graduated, I was diagnosed with osteogenic sarcoma— bone cancer in my right femur. It's a rare form of cancer, and I'm lucky to be alive. That winter, I had to start chemo, which meant I had to forfeit my job at the law firm. After a year of chemo, I had my first surgery. After that, we tried to get the cadaver bone to heal inside, but that was where the issue lay. It would not heal to my bone.

I went through three and a half years of different types of bone grafts from my left leg and my both hips. I was unable to bear weight on my leg and required crutches all the time. I also had lung surgery, during which I had a benign tumor removed. I dealt with all that from November 1993 through April 1997. Then I called Mark, who was living and running his healthcare business in Lafayette, Louisiana, at the time.

I told him that I needed to come live with him. Without hesitation, he said, "Pack your bags and come on down," and I did. Thank goodness I did, because he had me in the house with him and his family, and he made a phone call to MD Anderson Cancer Center. The next thing I knew, I was getting a knee replacement that corrected all of the other surgeries I'd undergone. Instead of trying to get the bone to heal after all these years, they were able to go in there with a knee replacement, a titanium femur, and I was walking within five days.

I started attending university down there, which was good for me because I hadn't had a chance to go to college. After my first year of college, I got a call from one of my best friends, who had just moved to New Orleans for a job relocation. He was working for a healthcare electric scooter and electric wheelchair franchise. After my second semester, I decided to purchase a franchise with my friend and open up a location in Austin, Texas. It lasted only eleven months. We just couldn't see eye to eye on some important matters. After a year and a half in Lafayette and a year in Austin, I moved back home to Dallas in 1999.

When I came home in 1999, I started working for my brother-in-law at a semi-trailer sales facility, which lasted about seven months. I was young, and I had hopes for the future. After bouncing around a bit, I landed a good job with a major tax firm in 2005. I worked there until 2012, and that was a blessing because the benefits were great, the pay got better as I made promotions, and the job was stable.

Losses and Gains

In March of 2011, my mom died, and that was rough. But Mom was a devout Christian who never wavered in her faith and never complained. I learned a lot from her about patience and love.

Although I appreciated my job and felt fortunate to have it, in a company of 130,000 employees, it still felt like I was in a rat race. In 2012, I went back to work for my brother-in-law at the trailer sales company and was much happier because I was in a better, higher-paid position than I had been the first time. Six years later, in 2018, he sold to another trailer company.

My career has only gone up since then. They sold the company on May 1, 2018. Today, I am the logistics manager for the company. We are a dealership for the semi-trailers that you see on the road, the big trucks. We're kind of like CarMax; we sell ten different brands of trailers and are the largest flatbed dealer in the country. We are also the largest Hyundai dry van dealer in the country, which is kind of a big deal. I believe the company is successful because of how they treat their employees, and I definitely feel my role is important to them.

My mom was always an inspiration to me, even though she was getting sick toward the end. I guess I've always really loved life, and I know she did. I've never understood people who have a negative outlook because they see others who look like they have more. I believe that you should look at the blessings in your own life, because we all have them. At one time, my own health was not a given, and I've never forgotten that. I get up early five days per week to hit the gym and keep my body in as best shape as I can. I also enjoy being able to share much quality time with my daughters, Ellie and Mollie.

We can have role models on the movie screen, but what are they worth in real time? When Mark Harris came into my life, he changed it for good. I can't express how much of a role model he was for me. Through all my surgeries, he was always there. He also had a good relationship with my mom. She relied on him to properly influence me, and he always communicated so well with her about me and about how he thought I was doing. He is definitely my number-one role model.

I have always admired the leaders and owners of the companies I've worked for. I make it a habit not to share in negative conversations about our employer since it hurts the morale at the company. Maybe it's because that was the way I was raised, or maybe it's just the way I am. Whatever the reason, it just makes sense to me to support the men and women who are providing a job for you.

If I could offer only one piece of advice to somebody else who was younger or just starting out, what would I tell that person? Magic Dust is that special extra mile we go for our employer, our team, our family, and ourselves. It's that quality that drives a person to go far beyond an average effort in everything they do. I think loyalty can be Magic Dust, and I think humility can be too. My advice, then, is *be* humble and *stay* humble as you succeed.

James Rodriguez

Plant Operation Director

"If I don't know how, I figure it out."

James was Maxim Management Group's corporate plant operation director for twenty years. A native of Nicaragua, he left when the country was in turmoil, and he was forced to start fresh in the United States. He and his wife, Miriam, have two sons, Allen and Danny, both mechanical engineers. He's proud of them, and I'm proud of James. He started out wanting to be a doctor but soon found out his true calling. He's wonderful with people, and he's living proof of how attitude can affect outcome. Here's what he has to say.

James's Story

By James Rodriguez

I come from a successful family that, back in the '70s, used to produce a hundred thousand pounds of coffee, as well as cotton, corn, and beans. My father was a dentist, but he did that work more to help people. He was truly into the plantation and being a farmer. When somebody had pain or a toothache, he took care of it as a service, but his passion was really about the crops we grew.

Then came the war, and we were told we had to leave the country. My father's good friend got us out of Nicaragua. We had to pay, and my mom, two sisters, and I ended up with my mom's family in Southern California, waiting for the war to pass. After three months, my mom got worried and decided to put me in a boarding school. My older sister and I ended up in Mississippi at a Seventh Day Adventist school, where I finished my high school education. I wanted to become a medical doctor, but the war was still going on back home, and we didn't have the resources. I certainly couldn't afford Tulane University in New Orleans, which was my first choice.

Because I had few options, I decided to go back to Central America and study medicine. Life there had changed considerably. Although my father had tried to go back and harvest whatever he could find on the property that belonged to us, he discovered that our houses, stables, and processing plants had been burned.

With my father dealing with depression, I enrolled in medical school in Central America and was approved. The situation was impossible. We had the government deciding everything we did, and we had to perform free labor for the communists when we were not at school. When we got a letter from the government saying that we had to be part of the militia, I decided it was time to leave.

I returned to the United States and applied to medical school. Only then did I realize I couldn't get in because US credits were not compatible with the courses I had been taking back home. So much for medical school.

Two or three months after that, we managed to help my father come to the United States. Knowing I would need a different trade, I began studying. I took classes and learned about construction. I went to work putting in floors with some other guys. When that didn't work out, I got a job remodeling a little hospital in Baton Rouge. I guess I did a good job, because they gave me a supervisor position, but on a training basis. Again, I had to take classes. And again, I was fine with that. This was a psychiatric hospital. I learned all the requirements, including the safety and environmental standards.

When I was at work one day, I saw a group of guys in suits walking through. Mark Harris was one of those guys, and I soon learned they were buying the place. As soon as I began working for Mark, I knew we were a good match. He knew how hard I worked. He knew if I didn't know how to do something, I would study and find out how. Back in Nicaragua, I used to handle a lot of people on the farms. I learned to respect and work with them. I also learned how to earn their respect.

Later, I learned that the hospital administrator told Mark I was the best one for a job Mark needed filled. The reasons, the administrator said, were my positive attitude and my willingness to give everything to do whatever needed to be done. I'm a problem-solving guy. When I've got a problem, even if I don't have the answer, I figure out how to solve it. I used to go to libraries, but then the internet came along and made tough situations easier to figure out.

I guess the admin did a good job of convincing him, because less than a year after I went to work for Mark, he told me he was opening a new hospital in Houston and planned to move our corporate office to Dallas.

"Want to come with me?" he asked.

Our oldest was starting high school, and my youngest was starting middle school. "I'm not sure," I told Mark. "Our boys' education is very important to us and must be a priority in our decision."

"Dallas has several great public school districts for your boys' education," he told me.

Although I worried about uprooting my kids, I had to do what I had to do. My wife and I started looking for schools. We must have done research for a month, and we realized Mark was right. Now, our kids don't want to go back to Baton Rouge, and I know we made the right move for us—and, most of all, for them.

When I look back at what we accomplished, I realize how amazing it was. We opened the hospital in 2006. This was after Katrina, and I didn't know anything about Houston. I had a big crew working in the hospital, and after that, we opened satellites. We had another one in Lafayette, and Mark decided to get involved in two more. That's about the time we started with physical rehab hospitals, and that change really appealed to me. I liked the idea of making sure the people we cared for could go home and pretty much do whatever they did before.

Lessons Learned

My grandfather used to say everybody wasn't born to be a doctor. When I was young, I argued that point with him. Now, I'm living proof that God works in strange ways. At the time of the war, they seized all my family's property. They froze all the bank accounts. People we had helped in the past turned their backs on us. But that wasn't the end of our lives; it was the beginning. Today, one of my sisters works for the navy. The other married an engineer and lives in Baton Rouge. My family is still successful in many ways.

I admire someone who can imagine both their current and future lives. Sometimes you hire people who aren't really sure what job you're hiring them for.

"These are the qualifications," you say.

And they respond, "Yeah, yeah, yeah."

I always ask what the person is looking for. "What do you imagine you're supposed to be doing?" They've got to see it if they are going to be able to do the job.

My wife, Miriam, came from Puerto Rico and works in healthcare management. Both of my sons are engineers. The only thing I ask them is what they see themselves doing in the future. That's the same thing I ask the people I hire.

I grew up going to church every Sunday, and so did my kids. I admire Jesus Christ. I tell my kids Jesus Christ gave his life for us and for mankind. I've tried to teach them the same values my parents taught me. I've done that by exposing them, from an early age, to church and to the value of a strong education. All the money I earned when they were young went first to making sure my kids got the best education, even at private schools in Louisiana. If I had to work extra hours or on weekends, I did it. I would do it again.

Finding Inspiration

I read a lot. I research on the internet. I definitely admire Mark Harris, and not just because of his success in business. Through all these years, I've seen the love he gives his kids, and his kids love him back. He will do anything for them.

Some people are born to do things. I can tell you that. Play sports with your kids, and you can see their interest right away. Some people are born with natural talents, and other people must study and develop a skill. When I was in medical school, I could see the differences among my peers. A surgeon has to imagine what's going to happen in the surgery before he starts. That's truly a gift. It starts with your imagination and obvious God-given intelligence.

Good people finish first—if they work hard for it. Everything you do, you have to work for. You've also got to keep your karma straight. If you do good by treating others with respect, it's going to follow you.

If I were going to give advice to a younger person or even my younger self, here's what I'd say: life is not easy. When things are tough, don't give up. There's a solution for every problem as long as you have faith in God and Jesus Christ. With faith, you can solve any problem. There's always a light at the end of the tunnel.

19

Brian Slipperjack-
Baskatawang

Guide

"Start simple, and have patience."

One of the beautiful things about Magic Dust qualities is the many forms they can take. You may have a warrior with both charisma and dedication—the same qualities you might also find in a motivator, implementor, or visionary. The combinations—some predictable and many surprising—are what create the inspiring individuals I am profiling in this book.

When I think about Brian, I think about connection, and, of course, I think about nature.

Fish Whisperer

As I write this book, Brian is forty-six, a grandfather, and he has lived a life few can imagine. Like his father before him, he is a trapper in Northern Ontario. When he was eighteen, Brian left the bush, attended and graduated from college, and became a certified welder. However, his spirit belonged far away from the city, and he returned to his tribal territory. His reservation is on the other side of Whitewater Lake, opposite the lodge, and he is closely attached to his tribe and his people. He hunts in the fall and is a fish guide in the summer. He tracks moose and elk, and he sees caribou miles before they appear to anyone else. I like to call him the fish whisperer, but his sensitivity and respect for nature go far beyond that.

"I love guiding and being in the outdoors," he said. "I love being home."

About eight years before I started this book, I was on a fishing trip at the Whitewater Lodge with my son, Tanner, who was twelve at the time. It's a good thing my son and I weren't paid by how many fish we were catching that day, or we would have been broke. The guide we had wasn't having much luck either, and somebody at the lodge suggested Brian.

When we first met him, he was quiet and would not offer much in conversation. We said we wanted to catch fish, and he said, in his quiet way, "I can show you a few places." Our moods improved right along with our luck.

Ask Brian if we had a good fishing day, and he will reply, "Yes." And then he will add, "Everybody does."

I knew Brian would be the guide I always requested in the future. We really hit it off, and we were together on that boat for five days and back at our cabin at night, playing cards, telling stories, getting to know each other, and bonding. My son was amazed when he took us to his native camp grounds and continued to share information about his life on the lake.

Bear and Eagle

On another trip, there were eleven of us in total: four friends of mine, their four sons, my son Tanner, and Tom Udstuen. On this trip, we were in one of our cabins, playing cards. Brian was our guide and was in our cabin when he stopped and said he smelled a bear. Three minutes later, sure enough, we looked outside and saw a bear standing on two feet, trying to crawl into the bait shop. The bear proceeded toward the lodge where we ate our food—and where the kitchen was located. We could hear the bear knocking things over and shaking the back door. He was obviously hungry.

We looked out the window, and there he was, just fifteen feet from us—not a mile away, but right there. After he attempted to climb on top of the bait shop, we could clearly see that he was at least seven feet tall, not to mention aggressive. Once he broke into the lodge, we all pretty much freaked out. Needless to say, everyone bolted themselves in their cabins that night, and I doubt that any of us got much sleep.

Brian climbed in his boat and returned to his tribe, where he asked for and received permission to put the bear down if he had to. He returned with a rifle and did so before the bear could harm us or anyone else.

So, that's my Brian bear story. Here's a happier one. It's the Brian eagle story.

While my son and I were out fishing with him, Brian said, "Hey, there's an eagle that's been watching us the whole time."

He would know that, of course, and he would also know that it was the same eagle.

He told us the bald eagle was his friend, and he also told us the bird was hungry. Then he did the most amazing thing. It still makes me shake my head when I tell you about it today.

He broke the back of a fish we had caught, put the fish out on the water, and said, "Watch this."

The eagle swooped down and snatched the fish in its incredibly powerful claws.

That was amazing enough. But then, minutes later—by then, the two of us were taking videos on our cellphones—Brian wrapped his arm with another shirt and jacket to give him some protection. He pulled out another freshly caught walleye and prepared it for pickup by his old friend. To our astonishment, the bald eagle acted on cue and shot down, coming right at us at sixty or seventy miles an hour. As that thing came flying at us, my son and I both ducked in the boat. Brian didn't flinch, and the eagle took the fish from his extended arm.

That's what an incredible sense he has and what a deep relationship with and respect for nature.

As you can see, Brian is more than a guide with an uncanny ability to find fish. He also proudly shares his knowledge. He could cast perfect shots under trees, and he knew how to feel the nibbles of each fish to tell us if it was a lurking monster northern pike or a school of edible walleye ready to become our shoreline lunch for that day.

During our first trip with Brian, he used a beat-up fishing pole with tape on it. Before we left for home, Tanner gave him a new one with a reel and a case to keep it in. I was honored when we returned and saw that he was still using that pole Tanner gave him.

Another trip was even more memorable. Tom and I were in the same boat with Brian, trolling against the rapids. Brian was busy trying to keep us in the middle of the rapids while Tom and I were casting into the rocks and flowing water. Tom was frustrated; his pole had gotten snagged on a rock, and he was trying to unsnag it by quickly jerking the pole left and right. In desperation, I said, "Just hand the pole to Brian and let him unsnag it." Within seconds, Brian grasped the pole in one hand while controlling the motor with the other. He quickly assessed the pole, handed it back to Tom, and said, "You got a nice pike on that line; go ahead and pull him up.

To Tom's delight, he managed to pull his largest fish caught so far, a nice thirty-inch northern pike.

On that trip, Brian was also spitting blood.

"You're sick," I said. "You need to get help." Brian explained to us that he had been diagnosed with cancer and was going to let it take its course without hospitalization or assistance.

Tom, a cancer survivor, told Brian how going though treatment saved his life.

I can't begin to express how I felt when Brian later told me he was going to seek treatment for the cancer. He said Tom was his inspiration.

Another two years passed, and I returned with more friends: Greg Bjorsen; his son, Jake; and Jake's college roommate, Angelo Amato. I asked at the lodge if Brian was back to guiding, and they said we had been his last trip before he went off for cancer treatment on practically the other side of Canada two years prior.

Guess who was at the dock the next morning when we woke up to go fishing? It was Brian. He looked fit and was in such an optimistic mood.

That trip, we all landed monster pike between thirty-eight and forty-four inches long. More importantly, we made lifetime memories. And, yes, Brian's eagle also treated us to a flyby within five feet of the boat, providing an excellent photo opportunity for my friend Greg.

Whether he's discussing fishing or life, Brian's philosophy is both straightforward and profound. "Start simple and have patience," he says. "Things don't work out the way they should when you're in a rush."

"Fishing is like life in many ways," he says. "Live the moment."

I consider myself blessed to be able to share experiences in nature with a true fish whisperer who loves his native land and the smell of the wild.

EPILOGUE

Your Magic Dust

Magic Dust Qualities

Accountability	Empowerment
Character	Integrity
Charisma	Leadership
Commitment	Persistence
Dedication	Positivity
Determination	Resilience
Drive	Success

How often have you heard the following?

"It was magic." That game, that performance, that evening, that event.

"They had the magic working." That day, that night, that moment.

"Pure magic. How masterful that win was."

When everything aligns and all the pieces seem to slip into place, that's where the Magic Dust is. We all have Magic Dust elements in us. As the philosopher Aristotle said, "The whole is greater than the sum of its parts."

Before I leave you for now, I'd like you to think about Magic Dust in a more personal way. That is, the Magic Dust we all take pride sharing as team players—not always as superstars but as proud members of the team. How many of us love to high-five, fist-bump, and ring up a strikeout for our favorite team, our town, our heritage, our family, and anybody whose achievements make us proud? I believe we all have this Magic Dust, and as you have seen in this book, there are many ways we can share it with groups and individuals.

It's a positive thing, this Magic Dust. It doesn't require smiles, or a lean body, or sharp clothes, or an I'm-the-smartest-person-in-the-room attitude (thank goodness). You're already using it at home, at work. You're seeing it in the people you deal with every day, and hopefully you will now see their Magic Dust from a different perspective.

Magic Dust doesn't favor any gender, race, or age; it's not political. I believe focusing on it—and the people who embody it—is one of the best things we can do, both in good times and in times of challenge. Have we seen incredible amounts of people step up and share their Magic Dust during an unfortunate set of circumstances? I believe we have. My next goal is to share these and other stories of Magic Dust, as well as to discover some more along the way. This book is a first step.

I hope to help companies encourage employees in all positions to sprinkle and share their magic ideas. I hope to encourage more people who think they have a unique idea to submit their ideas to a possible Magic Dust idea box. If we can help any company get more employees to contribute by offering ideas, suggestions, and improvements for policies and procedures at their job, then we all succeed. We will see better work environments, higher quality output, and greater employee satisfaction and overall productivity.

We all start with something special. We may be born into different families, in different towns and cities. We may be raised in different cultures, ethnicities, and religious beliefs, and our perspectives on any topic may be viewed differently. We are unique in our DNA.

I hope this book has opened your eyes to the world around you. I hope you will gain appreciation for all the different people you come in contact with each day and realize what they contribute just by being themselves. We all know the highly publicized success stories. In sports, it's almost standard to hear about a quarterback or running back who had a great game, including statistics highlights. Each thanks his team for the great blocks that enabled him to find the holes to run untouched, or the extra time that allowed him to find the open receivers. The concept of Magic Dust includes this team approach and goes even beyond.

I hope this book inspires parents to sprinkle your Magic Dust over your family, to sit together and share a meal, to ask about each other's day, to tuck your kids in bed and say, "I love you." (Say it a lot!) If you're married, I hope you'll take a moment each morning to thank your spouse and to send that person off by saying something like, "Have a great day today! I will see you tonight." Yes, the simple things are still the key to finding and sharing your own Magic Dust.

This Magic Dust is not a rabbit pulled out of a hat or a coin found behind the ear. It's many things and takes many forms. It's the Cubs, who won a World Series victory after one hundred years of heartache. It's the story of a Cinderella company being saved from bankruptcy and experiencing a turnaround success—like Steve Jobs at Apple. It's also as simple (and magical) as when our kids are struggling in school, then suddenly the lightbulb turns on in their heads and they start acing those tests! Was it really magic? That lightbulb probably came on after practicing, tutorials, and extra time studying, which helped the Magic Dust come out.

So, I'd like you to ask yourself this: What is your Magic Dust? What can you do to make your own life and the lives of those around you sparkle?

Spreading magic is habit forming. It's also contagious. As you are more mindful of your own outstanding qualities and make an effort to share your gifts, don't be surprised when you see others doing the same.

This book is just the beginning. My hope is that it leads to more magic moments for you and everyone around you. Magic moments add up to magic days and weeks—a magic lifetime. That is what I wish for you.

ACKNOWLEDGMENTS

I feel blessed to have had so many positive people in my life. I have learned so much just watching great mentors in life—from their leadership in friendship, family, and the workplace. I want to offer my appreciation to all of them. I hope by sharing a few of their stories in this book, I can inspire and motivate others and pay forward the lessons they have taught me.

A special thanks to Brown Books Publishing Group for leading me through the publication process. From the first day I walked into Milli Brown's conference room and she started grilling me about my ideas for this book, I knew I was with the right publisher. Milli takes such pride in her authors and the company she has built. She also made the introduction to Bonnie Hearn Hill, who was responsible for getting my ideas into writing and worked tirelessly interviewing all the people in this book.

An additional thanks to Solomon Gill, who kept me focused on tasks and deadlines while coordinating the hours of interviews required for this book, and an extra one to my daughter, Zoe Harris, for her support in reading hours of drafts for her dad.

Nobody has a perfect life, and our stories about Magic Dust come from all kinds. Thanks to everyone who shared and assisted in the creation of this book as we explored and defined our individual qualities to make a new Magic Dust in our lives.

@MENTIONS

Mark Cuban
Chapter 1

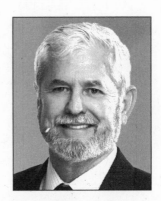

Paul Herchman
Chapter 2

Stephanie Nunez
Chapter 4

Elizabeth Bennett
Chapter 5

Charles Pierson
Chapter 6

Greg Bjornsen
Chapter 6

Steve Knox
Chapter 7

Jim Kelly
Chapter 8

Doug Dawson
Chapter 9

Hal Garwood
Chapter 10

Beau Williford
Chapter 11

Erin Young Garrett
Chapter 12

Colin Boddicker
Chapter 13

Debbra and Greg Raymer
Chapters 14 and 15

Abbie Harris
Chapter 16

Dr. Mike Judice
Chapter 16

Tom Udstuen
Chapter 17

James Rodriguez
Chapter 18

Brian Slipperjack-Baskatawang
Chapter 19

+ ABOUT the AUTHOR

Mark Harris was born and raised in the farmlands of Iowa with parents who espoused the conviction that nothing is free, so you need to work for what you get, but if you do, nothing is impossible. Through high school and college football, Mark learned leadership, team building, and the importance of character, but when an unforeseen career-ending injury left him with no option but to change his plans, Mark also learned how a life can pivot on a moment, leading to unforeseen heights.

With a degree in business administration from Coe College, Mark immediately packed his bags and drove to Dallas, Texas. His business career began with early mentors who have proven to be very successful business stories themselves. Mark Cuban gave Harris a blueprint of motivation and vision to follow, and later, Paul Herchman inspired in him an enthusiasm for healing with innovation in healthcare delivery services. Mark saw an opportunity in the specialty healthcare space and spent a twenty-five-year career building hospital leadership teams in over thirty different independent markets to provide care for patients requiring his hospital services. Mark completed his master's in health services administration from Central Michigan University and managed to raise a family of five children while creating over 3,500 jobs in his facilities.

Mark thrived on the responsibility of working with physicians, therapists, social workers, nurses, administrative support services, and others—the hundreds of people he had on payroll at one point or another. He made saving lives and providing quality patient care his passion. But when he got home, he was even more excited to be "Dad."

Mark's children, Morgan, Zoe, Abbie, Tanner, and Sophie, are all enthusiastic, open-minded, strong-willed, fun, and active people. They are his greatest accomplishment and his greatest pride, and he looks forward to discovering the unique kinds of Magic Dust each of them will bring to the world.